PORTRAIT OF
VICTORY
CHICAGO BEARS 1985

Kevin Lamb

A National Football League Book
Prepared and Produced for Final Four Publications

Prepared and produced by the Creative Services
Division of NFL Properties, Inc., for Final Four
Publications, 39 West, 300 North, Provo, Utah 84601,
David E. Treanor, President; Richard D. Treanor,
Vice President.

The names, helmet designs, and uniforms of the
NFL Member Clubs are registered in the U.S.
Patent & Trademark Office.

Printed and bound by
R.R. Donnelley & Sons Company, U.S.A.

First printing, May 1986

1   2   3   4   5   6   7   8   9   10

Library of Congress Catalog Card Number: 86-60945
ISBN: 0-934187-03-7

Creative Director: David Boss
General Manager: Bill Barron
Editor-in-Chief: John Wiebusch
Managing Editor: Chuck Garrity, Sr.
Associate Editor: Jeff Fellenzer
Art Director: Glen Iwasaki
Art Assistants: Laurel Burden, Mea Fred
Director-Manufacturing: Dick Falk
Manager-Print Services: Tina Thompson
Manager-Production Services: Jere Wright
Director-Publishing Operations: Scott Kabak

Contents

Men of Chicago

THE BIG, BAD, BEARS

America's Team?
America's Dream!

Only on the Bears would the glamorous quarterback play straight man for a pudgy defensive lineman on a national television commercial. The nation couldn't get enough of the 1985 Bears, and one reason was that people haven't had enough chances lately to say, "Only in America." Boots don't even have straps anymore, but there go the Bears, pulling themselves up from a 3-7 start two years ago to the top of pro football.

They went 18-1 and won the most lopsided Super Bowl ever, but they never lost their underdog appeal. They gave hope to the lineman in everyone whose only chauffeur is the bus driver, who only invests in commodities futures for tonight's dinner, who still believes elbow grease should take a person further than greasing palms. They brought America's old values back to life.

They had so much fun doing it, too. William Perry was their Falstaff, the great, big belly laugh of a happening, but even the main players did their jobs with as much relish as flourish. They were fun to watch. All season, the Bears swallowed teams whole, belched without apologizing, and reached for seconds.

There was something almost virtuous about the way they did it. Detroit quarterback Eric Hipple praised them for not going after his injured knee. "We just want to be known as clean guys who will knock your block off," linebacker Mike Singletary said.

The Bears were modern-day Robin Hoods, a vicarious thrill for everyone who has wanted to slap a rude sales clerk or strangle a bureaucrat with his own red tape.

They not only won games, they won them with a distinctive style. Even winning teams seem to look alike these days. Fans get enough monotony in their automated, commercially homogenized lives. They yearned to embrace heroes with eccentricities. The Bears accommodated them.

They had a quarterback with a punk haircut, who rolled up his sleeves like an offensive lineman, and spat at authority, wearing a headband promoting a sporting goods manufacturer. "Wearing a headband as a commercial will cost you $5,000," the Commissioner told him. So Jim McMahon wore the Commissioner's name on his headband instead.

Chicago had a 308-pound rookie defensive tackle whose coach dared to make him a fullback and whose charm made him a folk hero. Week by week, Refrigerator Perry added new wrinkles to his comic interludes that helped win games. He made the Bears cuddly as well as grizzly.

They had a Pro Football Hall of Famer who set running records

as fast as he pulled pranks. In his eleventh season, Walter Payton became a symbol of patience rewarded.

They had young offensive linemen who called themselves the "Black and Blues Brothers," palled around with the quarterback, and sometimes yelled back at him. They would drive for a touchdown, line up for the extra point, then start screaming at each other as if they hadn't done anything right. "The other team couldn't believe it," guard Kurt Becker said.

The Bears had a defense that expected to outscore its opponent and often did. They were good and they knew it, and they didn't care who they offended saying so.

They had an Ivy League-proper president with disdain for those who would "standardize and smooth out all the rough edges." If the players produced, Mike McCaskey said, "Football ought to be a place where eccentricity can flourish. What should be at the heart of what we give the fans is a vibrant, fun game."

They were allowed to be themselves—a radical concept. Most coaches feel the need to hammer their square pegs with dress codes and grass drills until they fit in the round holes. Mike Ditka didn't confuse team unity with team uniformity. "I don't want a bunch of clones," said the Bears' head coach.

"This is a bunch of looney tunes," wide receiver Ken Margerum said. "It's a bunch of selfish players who all got together and decided to be selfish for the team first."

The formula made football worth watching again for countless fans who could take it or leave it. The Bears set the Monday night TV ratings record in Miami. Their Super Bowl had the largest audience of any television program in history. They were the team people pulled for when their favorites weren't playing.

NFL Films never had tried to distribute a video cassette of a team's season three weeks before the Super Bowl. It did for the Bears because the one video doubled its sales inventory.

Another phenomenon, "The Super Bowl Shuffle," a rap song featuring 10 Bears with 14 backups, resulted in nearly one million records and tapes, plus 200,000 videos, second only to Michael Jackson's "Thriller" in all-time video-cassette sales.

For the first time in recent memory, Dallas Cowboys paraphernalia was not the NFL's best seller. The Bears beat them, with The Fridge leading the way. Orders came from all over America.

The Bears resisted the America's Team label. It had been too closely associated with the Cowboys' computer punch cards. This was a different kind of team. This was America's *Dream*.

"I think people around the country are starting to appreciate the Bears," Ditka said in November. "I don't think we play the same brand of football as everybody, but I think we play a good brand of football. It's kind of a fun brand. It's old-fashioned. It's hard-nosed. It's rock-'em, sock-'em."

It wasn't for everybody, he said. But it was perfect for Chicago, which always did hold middle linebackers in higher esteem than quarterbacks. "I think we'd probably fit in more in Brooklyn, Pittsburgh, Scranton, Birmingham...." Ditka said. "Good areas. Good work areas where people know what it's all about."

In case anyone had missed his point, Ditka said before the NFC Championship Game, "There are teams that are fair-haired and there are teams that aren't. There are teams named Smith and teams named Grabowski. We're a Grabowski."

When the season began, the Bears rallied around the memory of their NFC Championship Game loss at San Francisco, 23-0 the previous January. "We were embarrassed," Singletary said.

They spent the season exorcising demons of past losing seasons, past conservative offenses. "We're on a mission," Otis Wilson kept saying. Even when they were 8-0, Dan Hampton said, "We're a team with something to prove." At 10-0, they talked about the "opportunity" of playing Dallas. Never mind that the Cowboys were 7-3. The Cowboys were proven NFL elite.

It hadn't seemed to dawn on the Bears that they were, too. They remembered going 3-6 in 1982, 8-8 the next year. They acted as though they would have to struggle through a 16-0 season and a Super Bowl victory to prove they no longer were doormats.

And always, they remembered San Francisco. Worse than losing that game, they had taken it for granted. Ditka had told the players to put a chip on their shoulders in July and leave it on until January, but there they were, in San Francisco one year earlier, one game away from the Super Bowl, basking in the previous week's playoff victory at Washington.

"Last year, we kind of stumbled into it," guard Mark Bortz said. "We didn't realize exactly where we were. By the time we got to San Francisco, it was too late to see how close we were to really accomplishing something. Nobody wants to take a chance that we'll throw it away if we get there again."

If? Just a figure of speech. From July on, the Bears thought of the Super Bowl as a normal part of the season.

"I think a certain amount of cockiness and confidence is not bad," Ditka said. The Bears didn't cross the line to overcon-

fidence, except perhaps when players flitted from television station to shopping mall to car dealer for appearance fees before the Miami game. But during the game, their mistakes were of overexuberance, not nonchalance.

"I really think the players understand the essence of winning and losing now," Hampton said before the Dallas game. "We were a .500 team for years and years, but now the thing that really matters to these guys is making the plays and making sure we get a win each and every week."

If they looked desperate about making those plays, it was because, Bortz said, "There's a fear that if we lose one game, the whole thing is going to come crashing down." That drove them. When they did win, they were just as emotional about enjoying it. This was new to them. Gary Fencik talked about paying back IOUs to all the teams that had rubbed their noses in it. The Bears filled opponents' bulletin boards with derogatory quotes.

"We weren't so offensive when we were 3-6," Ditka said. When the Packers howled about his passing at the end of a 23-7 victory in their first meeting, Ditka said, "If they don't like it, let them do something about it in two weeks."

"We can get ticked off, too," Wilson said. "The way we get ticked off is with our helmets. We shut down a team's offense."

Much of that cockiness, then, was pent-up anger coming out. Who hasn't dreamed of sweet revenge?

"What are you going to do when you win twelve games in a row?" Ditka said. "Are you going to set a goal and then say, 'OK, we won't talk about this goal because everybody thinks we're too cocky or conceited?' If you want to do something in life, you better mark it up real high on the board and you better show it to people: This is where I want to be."

The Bears wanted an offense that could soar when somebody shut down their running game. "The way we won last year, we found out there's a way to stop it," Ditka said. "The 49ers proved that." They passed to jump up on teams, not just to catch up. They passed nearly as often as they ran on first downs. McMahon was the league's leading passer nearly halfway into the season and September's player of the month. A *Bears* quarterback.

They had the offense to come from behind by a touchdown or more in five of their first seven games.

"The thing that bothered me," Ditka said, "is if a guy wasn't wide open, we didn't try to get the ball to him a lot. You've got to throw the ball in tight spots." McMahon was doing just that—

and doing it often. "That comes with confidence," Ditka said.

The confidence became unshakable after the Bears beat three consecutive teams by a combined 104-3 behind backup quarterback Steve Fuller. That was when Ditka felt they could win the Super Bowl. "We saw the team come together as a team," he said. The offense wound up leading the NFL in rushing for the third straight year. It was first in rushing touchdowns and second in scoring with 28.5 a game. The team led in turnover differential and in possession time for the second straight year.

The defense had been superb in previous years, but it was hardly a rock as the season began. NFC Pro Bowl safety Todd Bell and starting linebacker Al Harris held out and never came back. Four of the first five opponents moved the ball shockingly well. Defensive coordinator Buddy Ryan complained he didn't have a pass rush without blitzing.

"What makes you so proud of this bunch," Ryan said, "is they started out so bad and had to claw their way up. They could have folded their tents and been a mediocre defense. It takes a lot of guts not to do that."

In January, the Bears' defense was being hailed as revolutionary. By attacking quarterbacks, linemen, and receivers, the Monsters of the Midway made offenses look helpless. They didn't have time to do anything. First downs were moral victories.

They held their last seven opponents under 100 yards rushing. They had the first consecutive playoff shutouts ever and allowed 3-for-36 on third-down conversions in three postseason games. They held 13 of 19 opponents to 10 points or less. For the regular season, the Bears' defense led the league in scoring, total yards, rushing yards, interceptions, turnovers, first downs, rushing touchdowns, and opponent's pass-completion percentage. It ranked third in sacks.

To keep things interesting, Ditka had to keep painting villains in the sky. He had a team that thrived on adversity.

Ditka created adversity, or at least causes. After San Francisco, there were the mouthy Packers, the Cowboys, and the ABC broadcasters who slighted both the team and Payton. After the last regular-season game, Ditka said they played so badly they'd be playoff underdogs. Wishful thinking. Before the championship game, it was Us versus the League. Commissioner Pete Rozelle had fined Wilber Marshall for what the Bears considered a hard, legal hit, and the team for wearing advertising logos. "We're not the image they want to project," Hampton said.

"Some people have animosity toward us," Steve McMichael said. "I would, if someone was out there barking at me."

Ditka had learned about creating crises from his former coach, George Halas. Another thing Halas taught him was tolerance. It had been hard for Ditka to miss that. He was to Halas what McMahon became to him. He criticized quarterback choices and said the old man tossed nickels around as if they were manhole covers. He understood as well as anyone that the player who cared enough to stand up and speak also was the player who cared enough to stand out on the field.

Maybe that's why Halas hired Ditka to revive his team. "I think he could see an awful lot of himself in Ditka," said Ed McCaskey, the Bears' chairman and Halas's son-in-law. At the time, people thought he had flipped his lid. Ditka? The clipboard thrower?

Halas had another cockamamie idea that winter after the 1981 season. Before hiring Ditka, he hired Ryan and the other defensive assistants. That simply isn't done. But when Halas did it, he made sure the two strong-willed coaches would have little choice but to work together.

Ditka has long since outgrown Halas's protective shadow. He has become more a symbol for Chicago than the Lake Michigan skyline. More than that, he has become a beacon in the national comeback search for the good ol' days.

The Bears and the nation both swaggered in tandem through the 1940s. They have spent the 1980s trying to regain the pride they lost since then.

It didn't renounce technology. Nobody can these days. In fact, the Bears' 46 defense recalled Halas's innovative T-formation of the 1940s. Ditka's offense had gimmicks that were called the most imaginative in the league, even without Perry.

But the Bears weren't a fancy team. They won their games by blocking and tackling. Even Payton, the most prolific runner in league history, could make a highlight film of only his blocks.

"I'm pretty basic," Ditka says. It's how he always thought of the Bears. Their basic style was one thing he loved about them even when he was in Dallas. Ditka can sound syrupy talking about how special he considered the Bears uniform, just as he can about hard work and teamwork. To him, they are all tied in.

"All I ever wanted to do was coach the Bears," he said. He wanted to make them special again to everyone, and Halas entrusted him to do it. When it happened, Ditka had one regret. "I wish he could see this," he said.

Mike Ditka

Head Coach

The Bears are Mike Ditka's team. Make no mistake about that. He gathered them to meet his standards and worked them into a lather with his blow-torch spirit. Funny how his fiery nature went from a tragic flaw to his greatest asset in 18 short victories.

He had it under control now. People suddenly wanted to know what Ditka *wrote* on clipboards, not how far he threw them. They voted him coach of the year. It was what George Halas had counted on when he hired this chip off the old cinderblock. Ditka would harness his flame without dousing it.

As a player, he had picked fights with teammates if he didn't think they were putting out. He was a perfectionist even in Little League, where he shoved teammates out of their positions if he thought he could do better. Which was always. If Ditka hadn't believed that much in himself, he might never have escaped the steel mills of Aliquippa, Pennsylvania. He never considered himself a great athlete. But he was All-America at Pitt, an all-pro tight end five of his six Bears seasons, a starter on NFL champions in Chicago and Dallas.

He grew up with solid, western Pennsylvania discipline. "There was a certain way you had to live, certain things you were expected to do," he said. "There was no maybe. There was no doing it halfway right. You did something all the way right."

He expected the same from his players. From the outset in 1982, he told them to play with abandon and anger. From whistle to gun, it was war. He said something else, too. He mentioned the Super Bowl the first time he talked to the Bears. They had thought it was unthinkable.

He remembered when the Bears felt they should play harder than other teams simply because they were Bears. He restored that pride. "He changed our attitude," Mike Singletary said. When others were happy about the strong finish to 8-8 in 1983, Ditka spat out the mediocrity like sour milk. The Bears had a right to win, too, he said.

Even in 13 years at Dallas, nine as a coach, Ditka said coach Tom Landry kept telling him, "You're a Bear. You're too basic." He liked the first sentence, but not the second. When he got the Bears' house in order, it would be bungalow tradition with solar-heating offense.

He put a wide receiver and a defensive tackle in the backfield. He ran from Shotgun formation, which he had urged Landry to install in 1975. "The Bears have one of the best special-play packages in pro football," Patriots coach Raymond Berry said. Ditka's mind was open. He asked questions fans would ask. What if William Perry carried the ball?

And he never forgot it was the players who had to win games. Not coaches. Not fancy diagrams on chalkboards. Landry has said Ditka kept reminding him to "rely on the player," not just the system. Give him responsibility and get out of his way, for better or worse, just like a teenager's parent.

Coaches can't help being father figures. Beyond that, Ditka is a mid-America identity figure, warts and wonders. Working-class upbringing, second marriage, smokes cigars, drinks too much at times, loses his temper. Also honest, hard-working, dependable. Landry is the Ward Cleaver none of us can be, but Ditka surely must yell at his kids. He just as surely cares about them, and his players, too.

He gave the Bears a dose of tough discipline and laced it with empathy and tolerance. He put Perry in the backfield to keep him from feeling left out. He tapered practice emphasis from physical to mental as legs wore out in November. He let outlandish Jim McMahon do pretty much what he wanted, as long as he didn't rob a McDonald's or throw away a game. His eyes could zap a Space Invader off the screen, but there's a twinkle, too.

The week after he broke his hand punching a locker, in frustration after a 1983 defeat, he told the players to win one for Lefty. The week after his drunk-driving arrest in 1985, he laughed when someone gave him a "Get Out of Jail Free" card from a Monopoly game. "It's only a game," he often says, and he takes it just seriously enough. Before big games, Ditka works more at keeping the players loose than revving them up.

But his temper nearly sent his coaching career up in flames. He honestly expected it would get him fired when the Bears dawdled with his contract renewal in 1984. The 3-7 start in 1983 had been the worst. The first year, he didn't expect much. The next, he said, "My expectations were too high." He took the losing personally, just as he had as a player. "You can't do that," he said. Coaches can't knock their opponent's block off.

It bothered him. He knew he couldn't expect those around him to keep their poise if their leader was losing his. On the other hand, someone suggested much later, how can those around him keep their fire if their leader loses his?

He hadn't thought of it that way. He didn't think of himself as the Bears' driving force. Besides, it didn't matter who got the credit. "Just as long as we win," he said.

Jim Covert

Tackle

Shortly before the Bears drafted Willie Gault to beat the other guys downfield, they drafted Jim (Jimbo) Covert to beat them up at the line. First things first. Coach Mike Ditka knew all about Covert. He didn't know him personally, but he knew James Paul Covert had grown up in Conway, Pennsylvania, 20 miles up the Ohio River from Pittsburgh. Across the river was Aliquippa, Ditka's hometown. Ditka knew anyone from those parts was more comfortable with dirt under his fingernails than with a manicure.

It's steel country. The young men go straight to the mills from their high school graduation, barely stopping to take off their caps and gowns. Covert's grandfather worked 43 years in the mills, his father 30 and counting. Both brothers and both brothers-in-law went to the mills. For everyone, it was that or a football scholarship.

"Working in the mill is a tough thing," Covert says. "You know your parents work hard for their money. They give that work ethic to you. Your parents want you to work hard. In school or in sports. They want you to do everything with your heart in it because the only way you'll get the good things in life is by working hard."

Ditka knew that. His parents raised him the same way. He also knew it was crucial for his rookie tackle to have that work ethic. Maybe more important than Covert's strength was his mean streak and his skill at pass blocking. Ditka was building an attitude on the Bears, weeding out the players who lived for payday. He was planning to add a lot more young offensive linemen, and this first-round pick in 1983 had to be their leader.

The left tackle job was Covert's the day he reported. There was no hiding that. The Bears had nobody else. Covert could have dogged it. But he couldn't have, really. Not any more than he could have tricked a 5-year-old out of a lollipop.

"He earned the job," defensive tackle Dan Hampton said. "He not only wants to start, he wants to be the best offensive lineman we have. That kind of intensity and competitive spirit was just what the doctor ordered."

So was Covert's pass blocking. Only three teams had allowed more sacks than the Bears in 1982. Two years later, when Covert was making all-pro teams, only six teams allowed fewer. Unlike most linemen, Covert learned pass blocking in college at Pittsburgh. He played left tackle there, too, the heaviest pass-rush corridor in a season in which Dan Marino threw more than 400 passes. Marino went down seven times, never under Covert's man.

"He'll do anything he can to keep you off the quarterback," Jim McMahon said appreciatively.

"He's got that good base," Hampton said. "A lot of the mistakes rookies make come from being overextended." They're so excited, they lunge into defenders off-balance. Soon, they're off their feet. Covert kept his balance.

Covert's initial arm punch, said Bears scout Jim Parmer, "stops you dead." In his second NFL game, Covert knocked Tampa Bay's Pro Bowl co-MVP Lee Roy Selmon off his feet with his hands. He didn't see why that was such a big deal. Wasn't that an offensive lineman's job?

Covert always has been very matter-of-fact about giving a runner daylight by pounding the daylights out of opponents. He prefers to do it quietly, then go home until it's time to come back and do it again. No need making him into some kind of hero. When Walter Payton said, "I don't know anybody who's better," Covert's expression said, "Aw shucks."

Back home, the Covert men don't talk football. They talk steel. "I'd rather just listen to them talk about this piece or that pipe," he says. When the folks gawked a bit at his five-year high school reunion, just because he played pro football, Covert said, "I felt weird." He wasn't special, he said. He had a gift for football. Without it, he would have been laid off at the mill, just like the other guys his age.

"Where I grew up," Covert says, "pressure is having three or four kids and being laid off from work. Hard work is being in the hot mill and it's 100 degrees outside and probably 140 degrees in there. Football's hard work, but it's supposed to be fun, not hard."

In his rookie year, Covert played with a broken finger. At least he assumed it was broken. "There's no sense getting it X-rayed because they would just tell me it's broken," he said. "I have to play anyway." That's what Ditka had been looking for.

The composure was a bonus. Ditka figured it would come. Pittsburgh guys don't ruffle easily. But Covert was still a rookie when an official called holding on guard Noah Jackson, and Jackson gestured to the crowd that the high-priced rookie was to blame. Didn't bother Covert. In the huddle, he was the one who calmed Jackson down.

The next year, Covert was an offensive captain. In his third, he made the National Football Conference Pro Bowl team. "I don't think there's a better tackle in the league," Ditka said, "and I exclude nobody."

Richard Dent

Defensive End

Even as a rookie, Richard Dent impressed defensive coordinator Buddy Ryan with his "good football decisions." If he had a choice to go to a blocker's right or left, Dent was uncanny about going toward the ball. He always knew where it was. On his sky-tipped interception that ignited a rout of Dallas in 1985, Dent was the only player who saw the ball.

"Certain players have an instinct," Ryan says. "They know when to swipe the ball away. I call them aware players." There are other great NFL pass rushers, but perhaps none with Dent's knack for knocking the ball away.

He made the New York Giants disappear from the playoffs almost single-handedly. Dent had 3½ sacks, forced a fumble, and stopped three runs behind the line. Afterward, coach Mike Ditka did an extraordinary thing. He virtually said Dent was worth every cent he was asking for in a long contract squabble.

"I think the kid has established himself," Ditka said. "I don't think anybody really understands the number of big plays he made. I know I'm pumping him up, but I'm happy for him. I like to see people achieve goals in life. It would be very hard to find a more dominant player in the league right now."

The Bears' defense scored six touchdowns before the Super Bowl, and Dent was in on all six. He tipped two intercepted passes, hurried the passer on another, and scored on an interception. He also forced two fumbles that teammates scored on, plus two others that set up quick, short touchdown drives.

Overall, he forced seven fumbles—a remarkable number—in the regular season, then four more in the playoffs. He was the most valuable player in the Super Bowl when the Bears took a 13-3 lead two plays after he forced a fumble by Craig James, the Patriots' top runner. He forced fumbles on successive drives in week 15 when the Jets were only seven points behind with the wind at their backs.

Need a big play? Dial number 95. "Most people say pressure busts the pipe," he says. "With me, it flows right *through* the pipe."

Dent led the league with 17 sacks, plus six in the playoffs. He had three sacks in two 1984 playoff games, when his 17½ sacks led the NFC. "Richard feels if he doesn't lead the league in sacks, it's a disappointing season," says cornerback Mike Richardson. He figures he could play any position, too. He even has intercepted a pass 40 yards downfield as a prevent-defense linebacker.

"Yes, I think I'm the best defensive end in the game," he said

casually before the Super Bowl. He plans to get better. Where other players are happy making the Pro Bowl, Dent talks about the Pro Football Hall of Fame. But there's no precedent for a pass rusher becoming so great so fast, with 44 sacks in just 34 starts over three seasons.

When he joined the Bears, he did one thing right. He dashed up the field in an outside pass rush. He did that well enough to set Tennessee State's career record for sacks, 39 at a school that had had Ed (Too Tall) Jones and Claude Humphrey.

There always has been resistance to giving NFL pass-rush specialists their due. The pass rush has become so important, it's like complaining that a home-run hitter doesn't steal enough bases. But Dent wanted to be a force on all plays. Until he was, he didn't start the first six games in 1984, his first of two AFC-NFC Pro Bowl years.

His speed is what sets him apart. Not only his first step off the ball, but his second step, getting away from the blocker. Ditka said Denver coach Dan Reeves told him he had "never seen anybody that quick that big." Opponents often say he's much quicker than he looks on film.

"If I'm coming off the ball very quickly," Dent says, "I get up on that offensive lineman before he has a chance to take a stand. He has to think, 'Is he going to hit me or not?' And then I can make my move, either inside or outside. But the main factor is coming off the ball, catching him before he gets back. Then he can't get set, so he has to hit you while he's moving."

Dent is 6 feet 5 inches and 263 pounds now, but Ditka says he's just as quick as when he weighed 224 in college. That weight, plus the half-dozen screws in his shattered forearm, discouraged scouts. But the Bears held their breath through three rounds without a choice before drafting him in the eighth round.

Personnel director Bill Tobin had a plan for beefing up Dent. He had seen his teeth. They looked as rotten as year-old apples. Dent didn't grow up with great wealth. He didn't play high school football until his junior year because he had to work. But the Bears could afford to send him to the dentist. It ended the continual toothaches that had sapped Dent's strength. Now he could eat well, with quarterbacks for dessert.

"It's something I like to do," Dent says. No, not eat. Sack quarterbacks. He's quiet about them, though. They're nothing to dance over. They're his job. "I like to do it and go back to the huddle," he says. "It's something I know I can do."

Dave Duerson *Safety*

Wilber Marshall *Linebacker*

Dave Duerson called it "awkward." When the season began, he was the guy who replaced holdout Todd Bell at strong safety. He knew Bell could be back any day. But when the season ended, Duerson replaced Bell again—in the AFC-NFC Pro Bowl.

It was only a little less awkward for Wilber Marshall. Al Harris, the holdout Marshall replaced, at right linebacker, hadn't made the Pro Bowl. Marshall was expected to beat him out anyway. Still, comparisons were his shadow.

Bell was faster and stronger against the run, Duerson was the better ball hawk. Harris was taller and stronger for covering tight ends, Marshall was faster and more aggressive. Defensive coordinator Buddy Ryan kept saying he'd like to use all four.

And Bell was so versatile. His assignments ranged from cornerback to linebacker. When he missed a game in 1983, four different people replaced him in various defenses. But Duerson had backed him up at every spot in 1984, besides playing his own Nickel-back spot. "I've been a utility man," he said.

The defense was different in 1985. "I don't think there's any question it's better," coach Mike Ditka said. Early on, its change reflected its newcomers. More turnovers, less flat-out, clampdown dominance. Duerson and Marshall each had five interceptions, Bell's career total and more than Harris's. "If the ball's in the air, I like to feel it's mine," said Duerson, who broke up more passes than Bell but had fewer tackles and sacks.

In the end, the 1985 defense had both the turnovers and dominance. "They make mistakes," Ditka said, "but when they do, here comes Wilber from the other side to stop a guy for a loss."

Coming from the University of Florida, Marshall had been tagged with the new catch phrase, "impact player." He almost was the second player drafted, behind the Patriots Irving Fryar, but Houston couldn't get an agreement to sign him. Pretty soon, rumors had him all but signed with the USFL. The Bears checked them out, found them false, and got a bargain with the eleventh pick. But they had to pay. The value of Marshall's contract was one reason Harris held out.

When he arrived at camp, Marshall was just another rookie linebacker. Ryan told him he wouldn't play much. Marshall didn't understand until he saw the playbook. Linebackers' assignments changed with each man in motion, and then *during* the play, according to blocking schemes or pass patterns. Looking back, he said, "The mistakes I made were so ridiculous. Watching them on film, I felt embarrassed."

The coaches liked that about him. He was conscientious. "Same kind of attitude Singletary had," Ryan said. "Asking questions, picking things up. He's impressive. He wants to learn. He'll be a superstar some day."

Another thing they liked was his abandon. "He gets there, and he arrives with a thud," Ditka said. Once in uniform, Marshall, normally reserved and quiet, said, "I get pumped up. I get emotionally high. It's the greatest feeling in the world for me. I just love to play football."

He wound up with more tackles than Harris had in 1984, more sacks than Harris's best, even at defensive end. Marshall didn't get a sack on the play when he decked Lions quarterback Joe Ferguson in mid-throw, but the league fined him $2,000 and enraged his teammates. Singletary said he would have made the same hit and proposed splitting the fine among the players.

But what impressed safety Gary Fencik most was Marshall's instinctive football intelligence. "He's the unsung hero of the forty-six," Fencik said. "He has made some right decisions that are uncanny, reacting to things I know he hasn't seen."

That always was expected from Duerson, a Notre Dame pre-law graduate. "What I like about him is he's intelligent and he's quick," Ryan said. But even Duerson went through an apprenticeship on the bench. It was especially frustrating for him because he started six games as a rookie in 1983 after two injuries at free safety moved him into the lineup.

"I came to camp [in 1985] with the attitude that I was going to win a starting job," Duerson said. "I didn't care whether it was at strong safety or free safety." If Bell showed up, he was going to play well enough that Fencik would have to watch out. But he tried not to think about Bell. "What I have to do is block it all out, just like the 60,000 fans at Soldier Field," he said at camp. "Todd's a great player. But we have a job to do this year."

He was willing to hit, if not as hard as Bell. He enjoyed that part, too. Not playing much in 1984, he missed the postgame soreness he called "sweet pain. You're so accustomed to it, you don't realize it's there until it's not."

Duerson felt the hot seat turned out to be an advantage for him. He was under scrutiny. When he passed muster, the opposing players and coaches awarded him with a spot in the Pro Bowl. But when it happened, he told the guy with the good news to quit pulling his leg. "It took a while to sink in," he said. "When I sat down to watch film that morning, I couldn't see it very well."

Dave Duerson

Wilber Marshall

Gary Fencik

Safety

Pigeonholes reject Gary Fencik. He's a head-cracking egghead in a world in which the two seldom meet, let alone in the same body. He's a football player who has an MBA and does ads for IRAs. He reads books without pictures. He likes music without words. He's from Yale, for goodness sake. What's he doing, throwing his body around on a football field like a tweed coat on a chairback?

He loves it, that's why. Fencik could quit playing pro football tomorrow, snap his fingers, and a line of Fortune 500 companies would form at his door.

Fencik had his taste of retirement in 1983. He pulled a groin muscle badly. Even his coach said he needed another week or two off. Fencik couldn't wait. He tried to play too soon, aggravated the injury, and missed another eight weeks.

That is not the act of someone who's dabbling in football to broaden his intellectual horizons. Smart as he is, he didn't give the long-term risk a moment's thought. He wanted to play. People read him wrong when they presume he's collar pins and wing-tipped shoes trapped inside a pair of shoulder pads. Fencik is both those people, but first and foremost he's a football player.

"If you're a football player, you lose some of your self-esteem if you're not playing," he said. "Plus, it's fun to play the game, have the challenge of making a game plan work."

Fencik doesn't deny the mental rush he gets from football. He's delighted at free safety because he says he was getting "stale" at strong safety until he switched three years ago. At free safety, he has new assignments, new perspectives.

But other NFL players didn't call him the league's top cheap-shot artist because he was outwitting people. He *hits*. In the bad old days of Bears' defeats, Fencik and Doug Plank amused themselves by taking target practice at enemy players. He has outgrown the habit, if not the reputation. He wasn't penalized for a late hit in 1985. But even now, he says, "When I have a chance to slam a guy, I'm going to do it. I guess I've always been aggressive. I like sometimes seeing the ball carrier squiggling for that extra yard, knowing that somebody's got his legs wrapped up, so I can try to get him and just bend him backwards."

When he gets a solid hit, especially in the open field, Fencik can't wait for his teammates to see it on film. His smart plays are expected. What he appreciates most is when either Otis Wilson or Dan Hampton, the defense's indisputable tough guys, "compliment me for something other than being football smart."

Fencik may have been naturally reckless, but after playing wide receiver in college, he came to the NFL tackling like a stockbroker. He worked at it. He still doesn't have training-film form, but there may be no better open-field tackler.

"Toughest Ivy Leaguer I've ever seen," defensive coordinator Buddy Ryan said.

"Tackling's mostly heart anyway," Fencik says. "I'm really proud of the way I tackled this year."

He led the team, an exceptional feat behind linebackers who don't let much action slip by. He broke linebacker Dick Butkus's team record (946) for career tackles with 980. Fencik also moved within two of Richie Petitbon's team-record 37 interceptions.

"He plays free safety like a linebacker," coach Mike Ditka says. "And he plays with the intelligence of a free safety. He has the ability to line people up and to cover for people if he's out of position. He's all-pro, whether he makes it or not."

He didn't in 1985, although he played better than his Pro Bowl seasons, 1980 and 1981. He's a big reason the Bears had the top rushing defense the last two years. Teams like to run at free safeties. As Eric Dickerson painfully learned in the playoffs, the Bears don't have a weak side against the run.

They used to call Fencik "Doom" because he groused so much in the bad days, especially about the offense. Friends feared for his career. Pro football teams might be open-minded about smart guys, but not about wise guys. But Jim Finks, then Chicago's general manager, understood. Fencik didn't have eight or nine years to wait for the Bears to sashay to respectability. He wanted a winner...and now.

As the team has improved, Fencik has come to grips with his brawnier side. It bothered him at first when all his Yale classmates were opening law practices, medical practices, or vice-president offices in respected corporations. "I was asking myself, 'Am I making a contribution? Is this really significant, the time I've spent on something I considered a lark, in a way?' But the more I played, the more I enjoyed it."

In his own way, Fencik needs football as much as the players who can do nothing else. Where else could he beat someone in a chess game and then clunk him over the head with the board? "It's such a combination of mental and physical," he says. "You prepare every week in practice. Then on Sunday, you have to react to things immediately with physical strength and mental agility. It's such a high. It's fun."

Dan Hampton

Defensive Lineman

It helps to understand Dan Hampton's relationship with pain by starting when he was 11. He climbed a tree to avoid his brother's BB-gun shots, fell 40 feet, broke both legs and an arm, and spent six months in a wheelchair. Telling the story, he can't stop laughing.

He picked up a five-foot alligator once, just for the heck of it. In seven years with the Bears, he has played with broken ribs, strained knees, sprained ankles, a torn bicep muscle that made his elbow a balloon, and a dislocated finger. The finger still is shaped like a forest trail, but Hampton is just glad it isn't on his string hand for the guitar he plays every day. When his back kept having spasms in 1980, he said it was "just some vertebrae rolling out of alignment."

He couldn't understand all the fuss in 1983, when he played a game 23 days after arthroscopic knee surgery. He had two sacks that day. "He's a little different from most people when it comes to pain," coach Mike Ditka said.

Even in the hospital, he felt guilty about missing a game. Two more operations later, he said, "It's like a toothache in the knee. A dull, aching pain all the time." But ask him how he felt and he'd say, "It's nothing, really." The thing that really hurt was seeing his name on the injury list. "That questionable-probable stuff is a bunch of crap," he said.

Players play. With Hampton, it's that simple.

Besides, Hampton said, "You only get sixteen days a year. After all that working and running and lifting in the offseason, you don't want to miss any. There's no way you can get to the quarterback sitting on the bench."

Hampton has the exuberance of a puppy, which is just what Bears scout Jim Parmer said he looked like when they first met. He wanted to be timed in the 40. "Usually, you have to track guys down and beg them to run for you," Parmer said. But Hampton had been timed in 5.15 seconds.

When Parmer clocked him at 4.85, the Bears made him the fourth choice overall in the 1979 draft.

They called him Danimal, homage to his 6 feet 5 inches and 270 pounds, his strength, and his unchained fury. He made the 1980 NFC Pro Bowl team at end, moved to tackle, then made the Pro Bowl again in 1982 and 1984. By 1985, his reputation was so solid, he made it at end, even though he played there only seven games and double-team blocking held him to 5½ sacks.

Defensive coordinator Buddy Ryan kept Hampton inside as long as his knees could stand it because he wanted him going to either side of the field. Even now, he's at end only a third of the time, in the basic 4-3. He still plays the nose in the 46, where it's tough to double-team him.

"When Dan Hampton gets on a center and the center doesn't have immediate help, then the center's got problems," Dallas coach Tom Landry said. So coaches find ways to help, but Ryan says, "When they double-team Hamp, they have to let [Richard] Dent run free."

When the Bears set an NFL record with 72 sacks in 1984, their only game with none was when Hampton's torn bicep kept him out. That week, Rams offensive line coach Hudson Houck asked reporters each day for a Hampton update.

Besides hurrying quarterbacks with inside pressure, he lets middle linebacker Mike Singletary roam on runs by absorbing several blockers. "Watching him from behind, he looks like a big shark going after some fish," linebacker Al Harris said. "You see a blocker and the guy with the ball, then Dan gets there and you don't see them anymore."

Hampton finished the 1984 season with 11½ sacks, but he also needed his third knee operation in 16 months. The doctor told him no running for six months or he'd end his career.

He didn't like it. "Laying on your back, watching 'Leave It to Beaver' and eating groceries, you go stir crazy after two weeks," he said. But it was time, he said, "to realize I'm not bulletproof."

The operations made him slower, but also wiser. He recalled the movie *Monty Python and the Holy Grail.* "This guy has his right arm cut off, so he says, 'I can still fight with the left.' He has his left arm cut off, so he says, 'I can still kick.' Then they cut off both his legs and he says, 'I'll bite you.' No matter what happens to me, I can compensate in other areas. I learned the inside rush when my right leg was hurt, and I used my head better when both were hurt."

On Sundays, he thinks of himself as injury-free. He cán't give the blockers a soft spot to pick on. He always said his success was more want-to than gift. "I just take the attitude, 'This is the line of scrimmage, and you're not getting by,'" he says. "If you get eleven men who are committed to that, and they're fanatic about it, crazy men, you can stop a lot of people just on sheer effort."

Jay Hilgenberg

Center

In a local automobile commercial, Jay Hilgenberg played John Belushi in a Blues Brothers parody. Good casting. He looks the part, with the same squared jaw under a round face. He even has the same incongruous blend of light heart and heavy mettle that characterized Belushi's biting comedy.

One moment, Hilgenberg wonders impishly how Joe Theismann keeps his eye-black so clean for postgame interviews. "He must have a mirror on the sideline," he says. The next moment, he mentions what a great way bashing heads is to vent frustration. "A lot of times after practice, I'm in a better mood than when I came to work in the morning."

The twinkle in Hilgenberg's eye never has softened the chip on his shoulder. He made the AFC-NFC Pro Bowl for the first time when it finally dawned on voters that the Bears led the NFL in rushing three consecutive years with yawning holes in the middle. But he made it by playing just like the free agent he'll always consider himself.

It wasn't always a source of pride. When nobody drafted Hilgenberg out of Iowa in 1981, he was steamed. "It was devastating," he said. The Bears called, mostly as a favor to his uncle Wally, who had played linebacker for the Vikings when the Bears' Jim Finks had been Minnesota's general manager. Hilgenberg told them he wasn't so sure he wanted to play for a team that didn't think he was worth drafting.

They let him cool off, then they signed him. But they never really thought of him as a starting center. He was too small. Even now, at 6 feet 3 inches and 258 pounds, he wouldn't ring bells on the scouting computers. The Bears kept bringing in other centers and eventually drafted Tom Thayer in 1983. But Thayer went to the USFL, three-year starter Dan Neal's back quit bending, and the Bears were "stuck" with Hilgenberg at center.

"I think free agents are treated differently," he says. "I think all the way through your career, you're treated different from a number-one draft choice. In every way. I think you tend to be taken for granted more. That just adds to my determination, I suppose. That's a compliment, being taken for granted."

The way the Bears take Hilgenberg for granted when they plot their running game, it's definitely a compliment. They can forget about the other team's nose tackle. Hilgenberg's got him. It makes the Bears less vulnerable to the 46 defense that spread through the league like a virus. The 46 makes centers go one-on-one, but Hilgenberg does it anyway. When he does it against a

standard 3-4, he frees the guards to cut off inside linebackers, which most teams use to chase down the runner.

"Jay's the best center in the NFC," says Steve McMichael, the defensive tackle who practices against him every day. "He's the best technician. He works hard in practice. It helps to practice against somebody who's better than the person you're going to go against in the game. Geez, the game's fun when you do that."

In Iowa City, Hilgenberg and center are synonymous. Jay's father, a former center, taught him the long snap when he was in junior high. He also taught his older brother, Jim, and his younger brother, Joel, who's now with the New Orleans Saints. "I think we're the only family that plays catch not facing each other," Jay said in 1983. Two years later, when *Sports Illustrated* attributed the quote to Joel, Jay shook his head and smiled. He's an offensive lineman, isn't he? He's used to being overlooked.

When Walter Payton gave engraved shotguns to the linemen who helped him break Jim Brown's career rushing record, Hilgenberg said, "I'd like to put mine over the fireplace, but I don't have one. Maybe when Walter goes over 20,000 yards, he'll give me one of those."

In the first Detroit game, Payton and Matt Suhey both ran for 100 yards. A big play for each of them had Hilgenberg making a deceptive influence block. "I'm supposed to miss my man. Just like always," he said. Don't believe it, said both guards. He did it just the right way.

For a lineman, the right way can overcome the wrong size. No blocker is strong enough to overpower someone 280 pounds. He has to use leverage, position, technique. That's what McMichael meant by "best technician."

At Hilgenberg's size, he has to vary his techniques to his opponent. He has to concentrate. Who to block, where to block him, *how* to block him, it all takes concentration. On Sunday nights, tired as he is, it takes nearly till dawn for Hilgenberg's mind to unwind from the ceiling to the pillow.

"If you're mentally prepared, if you're concentrating, and if you're fired up to play a good game, you're going to have a good game," he says. "Getting fired up should be no problem. It's your job. If you can't get fired up for sixteen games, you should look for another job."

Hilgenberg never had that problem. Can't even imagine it. "I came into the league wanting to prove they made a mistake," he says. "I never quit trying to prove that point."

Jim McMahon

Quarterback

To Jim McMahon, boredom is another defense to be shredded. He enjoys shocking people almost as much as he enjoys stunning them with a comeback victory. So he cuts his hair in a Mohawk punk. Or he looks for defensive linemen to block. Or he calls an audible that isn't in the game plan. Or he says something just to hear people say, "Did he say *that*?"

"Jim's not what people think about as a pro football quarterback when they're growing up," center Jay Hilgenberg says.

He is not Joe Montana, for example. He made that clear the week the Bears beat San Francisco. Montana is the standard-issue quarterback with the cool demeanor and the All-America image. McMahon would rather bob for French fries than have someone call him a standard issue.

"He likes to be disgusting on purpose," says wide receiver Ken Margerum, who has been McMahon's friend since before he was a Bear. "It gives him a kind of mystique. I think that's healthy. It makes it hard for teams to get a read on us."

McMahon doesn't *have* to deck out in such outrageous get-ups for television cameras. He likes chewing tobacco, but he doesn't *have* to use enough to cork a wine bottle. His eyes have been light-sensitive since childhood when he stabbed one with a fork when he tried to untie a knot, so he needs sunglasses for television lights. But he doesn't *have* to wear the ones with mirrors.

He *has* to be different, though. McMahon's costume might be a put-on, but it separates him from the standard issues. His fear of being lumped in with cookie-cutter quarterbacks is sincere.

So is his contempt for authority figures. Growing up Catholic and playing at Mormon BYU, McMahon had his fill of conformity and authority. When a Utah writer asked him for his fondest memory at Brigham Young, he said, "Leaving."

"That's why he's a great quarterback," Margerum says. "Defenses have all these computer printouts of what you're going to do on first-and-ten and second-and-long and third-and-three, but Jim just goes against all convention of what he's supposed to do. A lot of big plays go to a completely different receiver than the one that was planned. You can't defend that."

There's method to McMahon's madness. Acupuncture may have been just another stock Super Bowl controversy, but it worked. Wearing gloves indoors looked outrageous, but McMahon always did have trouble gripping new footballs. He likes to get down and dirty like a lineman.

"The big thing Jim wants to do is show people he can do it,"
coach Mike Ditka says. "(He wants to) get it done and win games."

The comparisons to Montana arose from their common flair for making big plays out of bad plays. "I think Jim free-lances even more than Joe does," Ditka said. "Thank God."

Ditka didn't always like that. "He was at Dallas a long time and he wanted someone like Roger Staubach," McMahon says.

Ditka didn't think McMahon spent enough time studying film. The kid didn't appear serious, so Ditka benched him for three games in his second season, 1983. It was a fatherly punishment, taking away the keys to the offense until he did his homework.

"He's not like most quarterbacks," Ditka said in 1985. "He probably is most unlike any quarterback in the league, but that doesn't mean he is not more into the game than any other quarterback. Some guys look at film over and over. I think Jim looks at it once and then he starts thinking. He sees it in his head more than he would see it on a screen. He sees situations flash, and then he says, 'If this happens, I do this. If this happens, I go this way.' "

McMahon calls audibles for the blitz even before the blitzer creeps up. He says he can see the look in the guy's eyes. He throws touchdown passes to receivers who aren't even the third choice in the playbook.

Ditka doesn't want to shackle creativity like that, not anymore than he wants to squelch the abandon that makes McMahon a training-room regular. "The thing about Jim," says Ditka, "is he thinks he's our best passer, our best runner, our best blocker, our best tackler. And he does it all at *his* speed, which is not good for a quarterback to do. He doesn't do anything halfway, and if you tell him, you're just going to get turned off." That's one reason the Bears have won 27 of McMahon's last 30 starts.

But it's also a reason he has started 30 of their last 42 games. He can overcome pain. He played with a broken passing hand in 1984 and suffered a near career-ending kidney injury. But he couldn't overcome the 1985 shoulder tendinitis that dropped him from the passing leaders and finally didn't allow him to throw. He can't play if he can't throw. He can't improve. That's why he played into his fourth season still with more promise than proof.

Just give me a full season, he said. That is his only goal. If he could have that, he is sure everything else will take care of itself. *Everything.* Super Bowl championship, all-pro status, passing title, diet cola commercials. Well, maybe not diet cola. Sunglasses. Better yet, Super Bowl rings. He doesn't plan to stop at one.

Walter Payton

Running Back

At 6:30 on the morning of the National Football Conference Championship Game, Walter Payton barged into fellow running back Matt Suhey's hotel room, jumped on his bed, and started biting him. That was Payton. Always playing, and, above all, a player. Not just a running back, a football player. And this was game day, Payton's day.

For three hours on Sunday, Payton can do what he does best without worrying about what the media does best. The two are at odds. The media creates personalities. Payton is a performer. The difference? A generation of kids thinks of Dick Butkus as Bubba Smith's straight man, not the standard for middle linebackers. Our voracious appetite for canned personalities has made television commercials a lofty goal for athletes. Payton is a full-color cinemascope with Dolby-sound highlight film, not a five-minute spot on "Entertainment Tonight."

Just watch him. Watch him turn and accelerate at the same time on a sideline run. Watch him bowl into a gang at the line of scrimmage and emerge from it five yards upfield. Watch him leave tacklers grabbing for air when he jukes on one play, then gasping for breath when he lowers his head on the next.

"Walter's the whole package," coach Mike Ditka says. "He may not do some things as well as someone else has done, but he does everything better than anyone else has done. He's the very best I've ever seen at any position."

It was ironic in 1984, when it took the all-time rushing record to call attention to Payton. He's so much more than a great runner. As a blocker, he lifts blitzers off their feet and puts defensive tackles on the ground. He has thrown eight NFL touchdown passes. He has led the league in kickoff returns. And Suhey says, "The strongest part of his game is pass receiving."

The blocking sets him above other great backs. He says it's the way he can show his appreciation to teammates. He's one of them, no more and no less. When reporters made a big deal of his waiting 11 years for a Super Bowl, Payton reminded them defensive end Mike Hartenstine was in his eleventh year, too, and safety Gary Fencik was in his tenth.

If he didn't block, Payton couldn't consider himself a football player. Not a complete one. "He's a guy who hates to be told, 'You did terribly,'" Suhey says. "So he takes the same pride in blocking or receiving that he does in running."

"Walter still plays like he's trying to be the best tailback in the tenth grade," Dan Hampton says. His energy could light up a town. He still works himself to exhaustion in the offseason. He doesn't have to, but he must. "If you don't," Payton says, "whatever you accomplish, you'll look back and say, 'Damn. If I did that, and I only worked so much, just think what I could have accomplished if I'd exerted myself to the fullest.' Why put yourself in that position? Just go ahead and do it."

One other thing the media prefers is dramatics over endurance. It bothers Payton more each year that he doesn't get his due, compared to other backs who have flashed and fizzled in half the length of his career. He led NFL rushers only once, with 1,852 yards in 1977, the year he set the single-game rushing record with 275. But he has cleared 1,000 yards a record nine times, and 1,400 six times.

"If you chart it, you see peaks and valleys," Payton said of other backs. "Whereas my career, I like to think has been like IBM or Xerox. I guess people have come to expect that rain, sleet, snow, sprained ankle, broken leg or whatever, he's going to be there. Sometimes you tend to—not knowingly—take things for granted." You do. Payton missed one game as a rookie and has played 158 in a row. He has made it look *too* easy.

"I think Walter's going to be one of those guys you really don't appreciate until he's gone," Hampton says. "A lot of people can't identify with Walter, because he's done things no one can do."

It's not just the records. They're hard to count anymore. He added the nine consecutive 100-yard games in 1985, boosting his career record of 100-yard performances to 73. His 1,551 yards ranked fifth in the NFL and increased his career and league record to 14,860. He had 2,000 yards combined from scrimmage for the fourth year. But what his teammates appreciate most is the example he sets, from the pranks that keep the locker room loose to the hustle that keeps them from relaxing too much.

Wilber Marshall remembered Payton helped keep his chin up through a frustrating rookie year. When the Bears won the NFC championship, Marshall said, "Walter was our inspiration."

A year earlier, when the Bears lost the NFC Championship Game to the 49ers, Payton was inconsolable. "Tomorrow is never promised to you," he said. "Unless you make the Super Bowl, you haven't accomplished everything."

He finally made the Super Bowl a few hours after he woke up Suhey on the day of the NFC Championship Game. "I'm going to take it all in and savor every moment," Payton said after the Bears shut out the Rams for his first conference title.

William (THE REFRIGERATOR) Perry

Defensive Tackle / Running Back

It all started because coach Mike Ditka felt sorry for a rookie who wasn't playing. William Perry wasn't going to beat out Steve McMichael or Dan Hampton at defensive tackle. But the first time Ditka had seen Perry sprinting 40 yards and weighing nearly 370, he told personnel director Bill Tobin, "Can you imagine trying to *tackle* him?" Hmmmm. He let the 49ers try at the end of the sixth game. The next week, a Monday night television audience watched with amazement and amusement as Perry ran for a touchdown and excavated for two more.

"I never intended to make him a national hero," Ditka said the next day.

The legend was off and rolling. Every time Perry touched the ball, the phones got busier. There were local appearances, national commercials, and umpteen-zillion souvenirs with his likeness. He appeared on magazine covers and talk-show couches. He was the object of songs, the rap singer of others. "They've got a movie on his life coming out," Hampton said. "It's called 'The Endorser.'"

"I'm just having fun," Perry kept saying.

He even scored in Super Bowl XX. It was his fourth touchdown of the season, including one on a pass and not including a near-miss on a 59-yard fumble return against Detroit. "At first I thought I was going to cruise in," he said of his long run. "If it had been the first quarter, no problem."

Besides being a national hero, The Fridge was a national pet. It's awfully hard to be both.

He made us laugh at the incongruity of it all. How many athletes do that? They make us gasp or cheer, rant or rave. Perry made us feel good.

He gave us hope by leveling stereotypes the way he did tacklers. He did what just wasn't done. "Every underdog in America identifies with him," Ditka said. "And everyone who's two or three pounds overweight."

He might have come off as a bully, the way he buried linebacker George Cumby of Green Bay on those first two touchdown blocks. Not The Fridge. He was *nice*. Gentle. Unassuming. He was the innocent country boy who stood the big city on its ear, but with his smile, not his leg-sized arms.

His ultimate moment may have been the attempted touchdown play in Dallas on which he picked up Walter Payton like a mother bear protecting her cub. It was a charming, unsophisticated thing to do. The referee also found it illegal.

He was wise enough to leave the gap in his teeth for cameras, to restrain his speech consultant from varnishing out all the "you knows" for interviews. That would have been like paving the streets of colonial Williamsburg. But Perry was not just another fat guy with something to sell.

To the Bears, Perry's value as team mascot equaled his value as team bulldozer. He was Baby Huey, a lovable cartoon character giving teammates a lift and defraying the media pressure of an undefeated season.

"You can't help but like a guy with his personality and sense of humor," Payton said.

As a defensive tackle, he was a typical promising rookie. He started eight games after Hampton moved to end. He had five sacks. "I have to improve on my pass rush," he said. "That's what the NFL's all about—get to the quarterback."

Taking him twenty-second in the draft was a calculated risk. Perry's contract would need a weight clause. He could have been a fat bust. Ballooning from 318 to 330 in a two-week holdout, he reported so out of shape that defensive coordinator Buddy Ryan called him "a wasted pick and a waste of money." Hampton called him Biscuit, as in "a biscuit away from 350." But Perry was so potentially devastating, Tobin said, "We'd rather have him with us than against us." After Green Bay, they called him Mudslide.

Perry weighed 13½ pounds at birth, the tenth of 12 children. "I was big when I was little," he said. He weighed 220 in seventh grade, 315 as a college freshman. That was when Clemson teammate Ray Brown saw him fill an elevator door and decided he was as big as a refrigerator. Even before Perry turned pro, life-sized Refrigerator Perry posters were hot sellers.

At Clemson, they told tales of his $55 McDonald's bill. Perry admitted to breakfasts out of a mixing bowl, 48 cans of beer after one game, dinners of "three or four chickens, no problem." His endurance waned with extra weight, but not his agility. He could dunk a basketball "any way you want it," he said. With a 22-inch neck and size 58 coat, he looked more wide than fat.

And he could play. As a senior, he was a second-time All-America and led the nation with 27 tackles behind the line. The Bears saw an earthquake of a defensive lineman, unaware he first would become the most versatile appliance since Veg-O-Matic.

"Nobody—myself included—would have ever imagined what happened with William," Ditka said. "The publicity and success he's had is unbelievable. The one thing that shows above all other things is the kid is a heck of an athlete."

Mike Singletary

Linebacker

Etiquette is important to Mike Singletary. He won't stand for late or malicious hits. He seethes at any suggestion the Bears take cheap shots. At the same time, he won't cheat an opponent by giving him less than his best shot. To Singletary, the hit is an art form, to be treated with respect.

"When you get a good hit, you just know you're doing it the way it's supposed to be done," Singletary said. "It's rare that you get the opportunity. You can't get the guy from the side. You may knock the crap out of him, but you'll hurt yourself, too. When you hit a guy straight-on, with good form, the helmet right where it should be, the right lift, that's thrilling. That's excitement."

Some people consider hitting the dirty work of football, tolerable for the chance to carry the ball or sack a quarterback. To Singletary, hitting is the good part that makes up for all those hours running on hills and squinting at film.

At Baylor, where he was Southwest Conference player of the year two seasons, he averaged 15 tackles a game. He had 30 in three different games. He broke 16 helmets. He can't explain the helmets. It still happens.

He's so intense, Otis Wilson said, "His eyes look like fifty-cent pieces." He has to come *down* before games. He listens to Bach and Beethoven. But after a big hit, he can't help grinning in the huddle. "He makes guys go backwards," Richard Dent said.

He gets hit, too. That's part of it. His answer? "Just bring it again," he said. "I feel if a guy hit me that hard, I want to make sure he gets some of it, too. I want to know he's feeling what I'm feeling." But the next day, Singletary wants to know he's OK. *Needs* to know. If there's any doubt, he'll make a phone call to the opponent he hit. Hitting and hurting are entirely different.

Singletary is quiet, deliberate, very serious. He's so religious, he listed God as one of his idols on a team questionnaire. His teammates were shocked when this scholarly rookie started bashing heads in his first practice, five seasons ago, punctuating it with excited growls. They called him the Tasmanian Devil at first. Samurai stuck.

He could have gotten by with just his Richter-scale reading. That's more than enough at middle linebacker. It was standard operating procedure for the Bears to replace him on passing downs his first two seasons. But for Singletary, it was waving a red flag. He had heard what he couldn't do all his life. His first coach said he was too small to play linebacker, the only position he cared for. Scouts said 6 feet was too short for the NFL.

"People are always trying to dictate what you can or can't do simply because of what's been done," Singletary said. He thanks them, though. "Every year, I wanted to get out and prove things to people."

"He *willed* himself onto the Nickel defense," safety Gary Fencik said. By the end of his third season, 1983, he was playing every down for a defense that puts linebackers in deep and single coverage. He dropped his weight. He kept receivers out after practice. He pestered defensive backs for advice.

"How can I improve?" He says it about everything. "I don't want to shortchange myself," he says, so he buys the best exercise equipment available. Defensive coordinator Buddy Ryan had to cut short their skull sessions so Singletary's family would recognize him. Singletary always drops by for the game plan on Tuesday, his day off. By Sunday, he calls out offensive plays before they happen. Knowing them, he knows where to go for those big hits.

But coming out of games really frosted him. Leaders don't miss plays, and Singletary is "the bell cow," as Dan Hampton says. He's the one who got away with chewing out players like a coach when the Bears slumped to 4-3 in 1984. They respect him. The night before the NFC Championship Game, Singletary's pep talk wound up with tables and chairs overturned.

The worst part about missing pass plays, however, was that every time he left the field, it announced to the world he was not a complete player. "I want to do whatever I can the best I can, better than anyone else," he said.

How was he going to be MVP without playing every down? That was his goal, as was the Heisman Trophy in college. Don't tell him linebackers don't win it, either. So what? He reached his other goals. Three Pro Bowls since 1983. Defensive player of the year the next two seasons. For 1985, MVP was all that was left.

"He deserves it," Ryan said during the season. "He's the best linebacker in pro football. He's the most dedicated kid I've been around, but his play proves he's the best. He can cover people. He can stop the run. He's smart. He can run. He's got it all."

He'll just have to keep improving, keep insisting they let him cover Willie Gault in practice. "I really feel one of these days I can be a great pass defender and great against the run," Singletary said. "That's what I want to be, like Dick Butkus against the run and Willie Brown on pass defense. I'm not going to stop until I get there."

Otis Wilson

Linebacker

When the Bears were shutting out Atlanta 36-0 in week 12, Otis Wilson was so excited to get back on the field, he forgot his helmet. Boy, this was fun!

Another time, in another game, a 6-foot 4-inch, 235-pound tight end tried to block him and Wilson knocked the guy three yards back. "He came running off the field and said, 'If that ain't the Big Hit Award, I don't know what it's going to be,'" defensive coordinator Buddy Ryan said.

"He's one of the catalysts," coach Mike Ditka said, "because when he gets excited, those other guys get excited. He pumps himself up to play and brings a lot of people up to his level. He shows emotion. He shows excitement. We need that."

Wilson doesn't hide his feelings. When he didn't make the 1984 Pro Bowl team, he felt horrible. He vowed to get even with the players who voted "every time I step on the field."

When they selected him the next time, Wilson said, "My heart just flew. You know that feeling you get when you're excited? It's like when you've wanted something under your Christmas tree and you get up and open it up and it's exactly what you wanted."

He knew he hadn't exercised political discretion with the voters. He popped off with his mouth and he popped them with his forearm. "Otis is cocky," fellow linebacker Mike Singletary says. "He's talking all the time. He doesn't mean anything by it. It's just his way of saying, 'I'm going to be here. When you come to play me, you better bring your lunch.'"

"Him or me" is the way Wilson plays. There only can be one winner, and he doesn't plan on being anything else. "When I hit you, I want you to feel it," he says.

When he joined the Bears from the first round of the 1980 draft, he boasted that he never had been blocked at Louisville. He laughs about that now. He wasn't blocked much his rookie year, either. Players don't block people on the bench.

"He was a rookie for a long time," Ryan said. "He didn't know what he was supposed to do."

All his life, coaches had asked Wilson just to find the ball and knock down the guy holding it. It was enough to be big, strong, and fast. Now Ryan wanted him smart, too. He gave him this huge playbook, and it slowed Wilson down like a ball and chain. "I was hoping he'd be more noticeable," former coach Neill Armstrong said early in Wilson's career, when he was tripping over his thought processes.

Ryan became his private tutor, explaining things on the prac-

tice field and the sideline, force-feeding him film in the off-season. "He has great ability," Ryan said. "It's just a matter of channeling it in the right direction."

Everything started to fall together for Wilson in 1983, and then it fell apart. A messy divorce destroyed his concentration. The Bears tried to trade him. They drafted outside linebackers in the first two rounds. Them or him, Wilson told himself. All through the next season, Ditka said, "He gets better every week."

"Instead of worrying about what I'm doing," he said, "I'm just *doing* what I have to do." His assignments had become "second nature, just like putting on my shoes. I'm playing ball."

"He's playing without any indecision," defensive tackle Dan Hampton said in 1985. For the Atlanta game, he graded a remarkable 97 percent. Ninety is considered excellent.

Wilson badgered Ryan to allow him to blitz more often. Pro Bowl linebackers were the ones who got sacks. Wilson finished the season with 11½, second on the Bears and fifth among NFL linebackers, behind four men who blitzed virtually all the time.

He also badgered Ryan to let him play every down, saying he could cover wide receivers as well as any Nickel back. "I'm not any good to anybody standing on the sideline," he said. By the end of the season, he rarely came out because teams were too wary of Wilson's outside blitzing to bring in a third wide receiver.

At the peak of his career, Wilson has a wake of fallen obstacles. Learning the defense, making the Pro Bowl, he treated them all like blockers in his way. Scars don't scare him. He beat the biggest obstacle of his life when he got out of the neighborhood.

It was the Brownsville section of Brooklyn, where junkies, pimps, and switchblades are everywhere. If you grew up there, you grew up tough. If you survived, you grew up proud.

"He's always saying, 'I'm from the 'Ville. I never ran and I never will,'" Singletary said. "He lives by that."

"Coming from that neighborhood," Wilson said, "you learn what you have to do. You learn to survive. I've been in some tough situations.

"In the neighborhood, it's either me or you. It's the same situation on the football field. I've always decided it's going to be me that gets the best of it.

"It gives you an edge. That's what you're doing in this business. Surviving. It's all about looking out for yourself. Keeping yourself healthy. If you can survive in New York City for twenty-two years, you can survive anything."

They Also Served...

Matt Suhey (26) takes off around the left side behind blockers Tom Thayer (57) and Keith Van Horne.

Looking back, it's clear the Bears stuck their chins out and dared to be wrong even in their personnel decisions. The scouts took calculated risks on draft day and the coaches took them in making their lineups. Enough paid off, obviously. "Not only have we drafted well, we're playing the people we drafted," coach Mike Ditka said.

In four seasons, Ditka changed 18 of the Bears' 24 starters, including kickers, and 30 of 45 players. Only 18 Bears played on Chicago's last losing team in 1982. But more than cleaning house, Ditka refurbished it. "It's not the fresh blood," Walter Payton said. "It's just the talent. Anyone can bring in fresh blood. You bring in a bunch of three-year-olds, and you're not going to win."

William Perry was the most notorious example of dice rolling on draft day. When the Bears took the most athlete available in the first round, critics howled. They said the big lug never would rush a quarterback unless the blockers had mustard on them.

Wilber Marshall was a first-round gamble the year before, when he was rumored going to the USFL. General manager Jerry Vainisi made some calls, picked him, and signed him.

Jim McMahon, in 1982, was enough of a risk for the Colts to take Art Schlichter instead. McMahon had a bad agent, a bad knee, a bad eye, and bad height.

Otis Wilson was almost the William Perry of the 1980 draft, but people are slower to joke about slow learners than fatsos. Defensive coordinator Buddy Ryan nurtured him into the AFC-NFC Pro Bowl, just as Ditka did with McMahon.

Mike Singletary was too short. He'd never play the pass, they said. The Bears traded an extra pick to get him in the second round in 1981, then watched him play every down as the NFC defensive player of the year the last two seasons.

Kevin Butler was more a shock than a gamble. Bob Thomas had set field-goal records in 1984. The Bears seemed to be throwing away a fourth-round pick. But Butler had the strong leg and unflappable nature Ditka wanted in a championship kicker, rookie or not. He was automatic from 40 yards in, and proceeded to set more records than Thomas.

Tom Thayer and Tim Wrightman had trampled the Bears' feelings when they bolted to the USFL. So what? They could help, Ditka said. He welcomed them as experienced rookies in 1985. The line didn't miss a step when Thayer replaced injured guard Kurt Becker after three games, and Wrightman wound up splitting time 50-50 at tight end. The way he dragged tacklers like a dog

pulling a leash reminded Ditka a lot of himself a few years back.

Thayer was a fourth-rounder in the 1983 draft, the one that put the Bears over the top. They also got tackle Jim (Jimbo) Covert and wide receiver Willie Gault in the first round, cornerback Mike Richardson in the second, safety Dave Duerson in the third, guard Mark Bortz and defensive end Richard Dent in the eighth, and wide receiver Dennis McKinnon as a free agent. All seven were starters for the Super Bowl champions.

Bortz had played defensive tackle in college. He was too slow for the NFL, but personnel director Bill Tobin thought he had the discipline to play guard. After his first season, Ditka boldly cut Noah Jackson, a longtime star whom he considered disruptive. Bortz would be better, Ditka said.

Players who make it big as late picks or free agents have something wrong that can be overcome, e.g., Bortz's speed, Dent's or Jay Hilgenberg's size, cornerback Leslie Frazier's injuries. With McKinnon, the problem was playing time. He hadn't hit it off well with Florida State coach Bobby Bowden, who had more wide receivers than he could use and didn't use McKinnon, who popped off more than most coaches like. He also blocked better than most coaches dream about for a wide receiver, and made the tough catches. Tobin saw that by watching him practice.

Richardson was a college safety who had the speed and aggressive nature to play Ryan's bump-and-run corner. He was given to lapses, so Ryan demoted him in the 1985 mini-camp. Ryan just wanted to prod him. "He's playing like he has something to prove," Ditka said during the season. "He's defying people out there." Ryan called him "a changed kid."

Gault was, too. In the playoffs, he was fighting for catches, something he hadn't done much of his first two years. But he was valuable even then. He caught the long ball, and his world-class speed made cornerbacks give Payton more room to run.

Gault had the blazing speed and college experience that simply aren't available after the first round. The Bears started nine first-rounders, tied with New England for most in the league, and all but three from former general manager Jim Finks's drafts, 1975-1983. They not only play, they play where first-rounders are needed most. Hampton and Perry rush the passer, tackles Covert and Keith Van Horne protect the passer. McMahon and backup Steve Fuller (a Kansas City first-rounder in 1979) throw the ball, Gault catches it. Payton runs the ball, Singletary and Marshall stop the run.

Frazier barely could walk after two leg injuries his last year in college, at Alcorn State, but the Bears needed cornerbacks badly. His speed had slipped, but not his relish for challenge. "In our defense, you've got to have people who say, 'Throw it to me,'" he says. Offenses preferred to avoid Frazier's zest for the ball, but he still led the team in 1985 with six interceptions.

The Bears stuck their necks out on veteran moves, too. They could have lived with Bob Avellini as their reserve quarterback. They won with Steve Fuller. Dave Finzer was a good punter. Ditka decided Maury Buford was better.

Emery Moorehead was a five-year journeyman at fullback and wide receiver before Ditka arrived. He needed a tight end. The Bears hadn't had an acceptable one since Ditka himself. What about Moorehead? He looked big enough, and he sure was fast enough. Moorehead put the tight end back in the passing game without losing anything from the run.

Ditka also inherited Van Horne and running back Matt Suhey, the only holdover starters on offense besides Payton. With talent, he was patient. Van Horne developed from a fringe starter to a Pro Bowl candidate, and Suhey stormed back from a sluggish 1982 season to average 4.1 yards a carry.

"They took a chance on me," defensive tackle Steve McMichael said. At New England, he was considered too rowdy. Tobin liked his rowdy playing and signed him as a free agent in 1981. Ditka called him the Bears' best defensive lineman before Dent caught fire, McMichael's knee wore down, and opponents wised up enough to double team him. His 26 sacks for three years were high on the NFL list of inside pass rushers.

McMichael might be the quintessential Bear—talented, aggressive, ornery, and just playfully eccentric enough not to fit in on a lot of teams. "If it weren't for football, I'd be in jail," he says often. At Texas, he amused himself by dangling people by their ankles from a bridge. He and Hampton, who is from Arkansas, once walked into a motorcycle bar, offered to fight the lot of them, and left in a huff when there were no takers.

McMichael has settled down since his recent marriage, freeing up barstools all over town and forgoing his usual summer rattlesnake hunt in Texas. It left him with more energy for football. "In the past, it was, 'Oh, practice is over. What can I screw up now?'" he says. But football always did come first.

"He goes full-bore all the time in practice," Hilgenberg says. In games, he's smart enough not to drain his energy by fighting.

He's smart enough to be Perry's personal coach. He's smart enough to appreciate that the Bears never went through with the idea of making him an offensive lineman.

"He's a throwback to the old high-top black-shoes guys," Ryan says, "to the guys who'd line up and whup you and didn't worry about anything else. It's pretty hard to get too many of those. There's still a place for them in society. Especially in football."

The Bears collect them. Their coaching staff developed a great team from them not only by being good teachers, but by creating an atmosphere that allows colorful eccentricities to flourish.

"You couldn't stand to have eleven outlandish players," president Mike McCaskey says. "That would be like a meal with nothing but pepper. But you're looking for character you can depend on when the going gets tough."

Ditka even has a weekly meeting for team leaders to air gripes. "When I was a player, I felt, if I'm giving my best and if I disagree with something, I'm going to say so," he says. "I don't mind disagreements. As long as everybody wants to make the Bears a better team."

Even when his defensive coach contradicted him, Ditka tolerated it. "Why shouldn't he?" Ryan said slyly. "I don't get mad when he disagrees with me."

Ryan was a boat-rocker, answering questions instead of weighing them, generally fitting in with football group-think like a Hawaiian shirt with corporate pinstripes. But he had the players' respect. When a questionable blitz call backfired, they blamed themselves. More than that, they had his affection.

He left an abrasive first impression, calling players by number and demoralizing epithets. "I really didn't like him very much at first," Singletary said. But he grew to love Ryan. "He doesn't just tell me I have a problem. He tells me how I can solve it."

To Ryan's innovative defense, Tobin, Finks, and Ditka added the players who made it spectacular. The great pass rushers, fearless cornerbacks, linebackers who run like safeties, and safeties who hit like linebackers. "You talk to other coaches, the first thing they say is we've got good personnel," Ditka said.

The players had something else in common, too. "There are people who run *to* the tackle and people who run *through* the tackle," Tobin says. Bears players run through it. As McMichael puts it, "All the computers and genius coaches aren't worth a thing on Sundays if you don't have a bunch of guys who go out and play as though somebody called their mommas a nasty name."

The 1985 Season

RETURN OF THE MONSTERS OF THE MIDWAY

Week 1

Bears 38, Buccaneers 28

Looking back, coach Mike Ditka would call it perhaps the biggest single play of the season. The Bears had fallen behind Tampa Bay 28-17 at halftime. They were off to a stumbling start, exactly what they felt was crucial to avoid. History says teams that lose opening games to division rivals, especially at home, hardly ever go on to win division championships.

Then, just 22 seconds into the second half, Chicago cornerback Leslie Frazier intercepted Steve DeBerg's pass for a 29-yard touchdown. The game was back within reach.

"You look for one thing to trigger you," Ditka said about the interception. "It shocked me when I saw it. I said, 'There it is. That was the one pump we needed.' "

Richard Dent had a hand in the play, as he would in so many big plays during the 1985 season. The defensive right end saw Buccaneers left tackle George Yarno's weight tip a smidgen backward when he lined up, the way a blocker does for a quick pass. After the snap, Dent drifted out toward the path of the pass he expected. When it came, he leaped for the ball. "I'm glad I just got half of it," he said.

Behind him, Frazier was sniffing out the same play. It was Frazier's first game that counted since the tenth week of the 1984 season when he tore ligaments in his foot. His foot had bothered him throughout training camp. But now, with a new pad in his shoe, he felt confident enough to break for the ball.

He was in the right defense, a three-deep zone. Ditka had urged defensive coordinator Buddy Ryan to use more zone defenses because they let pass defenders watch the ball instead of the receiver. He wanted more turnovers. Now, when Frazier saw DeBerg drop back only three steps and suspected a quick, sideline pass, he started moving toward the interception before the ball was in the air.

The Bears went ahead 31-28 late in the third quarter, when Matt Suhey dived near the sideline in the end zone for a nine-yard touchdown catch. Shaun Gayle blocked a Tampa Bay punt that set up the last Chicago score.

As the 38-28 victory wound down, tenth-year safety Gary Fencik and eleventh-year running back Walter Payton were trying to remember the last time the Bears had come from 14 points behind to win. It was 61 games ago, in 1980. Now the Bears trailed Tampa Bay 21-7 early in the second quarter. It looked hopeless. Reporters fled the press box to go see Pete Rose equal Ty Cobb's hit record at Wrigley Field.

The comeback against Tampa Bay was big news when the Bears were 1-0 and looking ahead, not 15-1 and winning a title. Their offense had bailed out their defense, of all things. This was the offense nobody thought could bail out a bathtub.

Ditka had wanted a better mix of runs and passes. He got 34 runs and 34 passes. Jim Mc-Mahon's 23 completions were a career high. And he put the ball in the air without putting Payton in mothballs. "Great game plan," Payton said after gaining 120 yards on 17 carries.

While the offensive players slapped each other's backs, Ryan said he felt the worst he'd ever felt after a win. His vaunted defense had let Tampa Bay's James Wilder run for 166 yards. He had been afraid of something like this when the team hadn't signed holdouts Al Harris and Todd Bell, both starters in 1984. The other guys tried to do too much, compensating for their absence. They were suckered by counter plays, rollouts, and play-action passes. "When you're being really aggressive," middle linebacker Mike Singletary said, "you have a tendency not to play very smart."

It was a good lesson, Singletary said. Maybe now the defense wouldn't take its superiority for granted. Best of all, the Bears had learned a new way to win.

Nose tackle David Logan of Tampa Bay pulled down Bears quarterback Jim McMahon (right). McMahon helped the Bears to a 38-28 comeback victory by passing for 274 yards. Pages 50-51: James Wilder burst through the Chicago defense en route to a stunning 166 yards.

San Francisco quarterback Joe Montana (below) burned the Vikings by passing for 265 yards and two touchdowns, both to running back Roger Craig. But Minnesota, inspired by the return of coach Bud Grant,

rallied for 21 points in the fourth quarter—including a 44-yard touchdown pass from Tommy Kramer to Mike Jones (right)—to upset the defending Super Bowl-champion 49ers 28-21.

Vikings '85

When Bud Grant resumed coaching the Minnesota Vikings, he admitted a lot of teams had more talent but said there were ways to win without great talent. Turnovers, for example. And kicking teams. Sometimes playing hard and playing smart can beat playing well.

Right off, he made believers of the NFL champions. Minnesota beat San Francisco 28-21 at home by winning 7-1 in turnovers. The 49ers, who had committed only 22 turnovers in 1984, coughed up five fumbles and two interceptions. They outgained the Vikings by 221 yards but blew a 21-14 lead in the last three minutes, when they fumbled at their own 1-yard line and then fumbled away the Vikings' kickoff.

"The balls were flying all over the place," said Joey Browner, whose recovery on the kickoff was his third. "Wherever the balls go, I go." Rufus Bess, a 5-9 cornerback, forced three fumbles and intercepted Joe Montana's last pass.

The Vikings' 3-1 start turned out to be false hope. Grant was right about their talent. They lost six of their next eight. But they weren't getting blown out. In 1984 they had lost six games by more than 20 points. Their worst loss in 1985 was by 20. The magic returned in week 13, when the Vikings trailed the Eagles 23-0 with nine minutes left and beat them 28-23.

The opening victory exorcised the demons of 1984, when the Vikings collapsed to 3-13 under coach Les Steckel and lost 51-7 to the 49ers. They didn't restore their glory years, but they regained their pride. Grant kept a career-high 13 rookies on the roster. After a 7-9 season, he could resign again. He turned over a promising team to offensive coordinator Jerry Burns.

Week 2

Bears 20, Patriots 7

It was time for the Bears' defense to stand up and be counted. What were they using? Thirteen men? Fourteen? "Wherever I looked, they had a person there," New England quarterback Tony Eason said after the Bears beat the Patriots 20-7 at Soldier Field.

New England spent all of 17 seconds in Bears territory. There were two snaps from the 49 late in the first half, and Eason's 90-yard pass-and-run play to Craig James that spoiled the shutout with 9:03 to play. Otherwise, Eason took six sacks and threw three interceptions, a career high. Sixteen running plays gained just 27 yards. This from a team that had picked up 206 yards rushing one week before.

Middle linebacker Mike Singletary had three of the sacks and an interception, demonstrating what makes the 46 defense so stifling. It has six players on the line. The only blocker without a helmet in his face is the strongside tackle. Two linebackers are on that side, Wilber Marshall over the tight end and Otis Wilson outside him. Usually, that's where the blitz comes from. The tight end can block only one of them. But the Patriots shut down the outside blitz by sending their tackle after Wilson.

So far, so good. Trouble was, the tackle left a gaping hole in the middle for Singletary. "He was coming free all day," defensive coordinator Buddy Ryan said.

"Mike was calling out some of their plays before they did," linebacker Wilson said. "One time, I said, 'Hey, Mike, do you have a crystal ball out there?'"

That's the other key to the Bears' defense. Besides being talented and flexible, it's well prepared. "All good offenses type themselves," Ryan said, using coaches' shorthand for stereotype and meaning they have predictable tendencies. And he said all along the Patriots had a good offense. Throughout the regular season, before anyone thought about the Patriots reaching the Super Bowl, Ryan kept maintaining that the New England game was the Chicago defense's best game.

"I haven't seen Buddy as enthusiastic about a game plan as he was today," free safety Gary Fencik said.

The defense provided the lift the Bears needed on a day when quarterback Jim McMahon's upper back needed traction and Walter Payton reinjured his bruised ribs. Payton carried only 11 times for 39 yards. But the game was practically out of reach as soon as the Bears opened the game with a five-play, 69-yard touchdown drive, McMahon hitting Dennis McKinnon for a 32-yard touchdown. It was McKinnon's second touchdown in two games on plays when he wasn't even the secondary receiver. "Jim finds people," coach Mike Ditka said.

For all the good news, the Bears were almost inconsolable in victory. They had blown their shutout. On offense, they hadn't blown any scoreboard fuses. Four trips past the Patriots' 20-yard line had produced only 13 points, a problem that would crop up all season.

"We had a pretty good day," defensive end Richard Dent said. "Not a great day. They had a couple of drives. We like to go three downs and out all the time. That's all the down marker reads. Three downs."

Even Singletary was disgusted with himself. He had bungled a chance for another interception. Singletary's nickname is Samurai because of the noises he makes in the heat of battle. When he was breaking toward the ball, his Samurai yells alerted James and he knocked the ball down. "For once, I should have just been quiet," Singletary said.

Being good was no longer good enough for the Bears, who considered such a status beyond their wildest fantasies not long ago. But that was not all bad. As Fencik said, "Our expectations are much higher."

Bears cornerback Leslie Frazier (right) leaped to defend a pass intended for New England wide receiver Stanley Morgan. The rugged Chicago defense held the Patriots to 206 net yards in a 20-7 Bears victory. Pages 56-57: Rookie Thomas Sanders (left) gained 37 yards in place of Walter Payton, who left the game with bruised ribs. Safety Fred Marion (31, right) was New England's defensive star with eight solo tackles and an interception.

Green Bay defenders Brian Noble and Ezra Johnson converged on Giants quarterback Phil Simms for one of the Packers' five sacks. New York's Ali Haji-Sheikh missed a 47-yard field goal with 1:06 to play as the Packers held on for a 23-20 victory.

Packers '85

The first week, the Packers looked awful in losing to New England. The second week, they looked splendid in beating the New York Giants in Green Bay. "This is a big boost," tackle Greg Koch said after the 23-20 victory. "We played a playoff-caliber team that was riding high." But the first two weeks were the story of Green Bay's season—8-8 for the third straight year.

"I can't change it," coach Forrest Gregg said. "I wish I could. I wish I could just snap my fingers and two games would pop up that we won. And then we all wouldn't be going home for Christmas."

As it turned out, the Packers missed the playoffs because the Giants were the only team with a winning record they beat. Their interceptions dropped from a fifth-ranked 27 in 1984 to 15, which ranked next-to-last. And they still couldn't protect their quarterbacks, who were sacked 50 times.

Lynn Dickey is widely regarded as one of the NFL's guttiest players. In 1984, he had talked of playing five more years. But he took such a beating in 1985, he begged out of the lineup twice. His enthusiasm gone at 36, Dickey appeared ready to turn the offense over to Jim Zorn or Randy Wright.

But there was reason for encouragement. Al Del Greco straightened out the shaky placekicking and won two games with last-second field goals. Ezra Johnson returned from three back operations to lead the team with 9½ sacks. The defensive ranking improved from sixteenth in 1984 to twelfth.

The Packers won all six of their division games that weren't against Chicago, and they were the only team to lose to the Bears by less than a touchdown.

Week 3

Bears 33, Vikings 24

This was prime-time television at its dramatic best. Where do they get all those outrageous plots, anyway?

Picture this: Big game coming up Thursday night. Chicago at Minnesota. They're in the same division, both 2-0. And Chicago's hot-shot kid quarterback gets hurt. No, not an incurable disease. Have him spend two nights in traction for his upper back. Throw in a leg infection, too. He's a feisty one, though. Keeps vowing he'll play anyway. Give him an Irish temper. Call him Jim McMahon. So when the coach benches him—because everyone knows a quarterback can't play if he's too hurt to practice all week—the kid throws a fit. Maybe some furniture, too.

The game starts and he's way down at the end of the bench. Pouting. His team's looking bad. It's down 17-9 with 7:32 left in the third quarter. The kid's in the coach's ear now. "Put me in! Put me in!" Coach paces nervously. Stops. Pats kid on rump. "We need you, Kid. Go on in and save the game."

First play, the kid throws a 70-yard touchdown pass. Second play, 25-yard touchdown pass. Third play, he tries for a 68-yard touchdown, but it's underthrown. The kid can't be perfect. Wait for the eighth play. A 43-yard touchdown pass. Now it's 30-17 and still the third quarter. The kid's team wins the game 33-24. Is that a concept, or what?

"It was like one of those old-time Notre Dame movies," Walter Payton said when it was over.

"Incredible," running back Matt Suhey said. "I've never seen anything like it."

"I'm just giddy," safety Gary Fencik said. "We've made a quantum leap. We don't have to hang our heads quite so far if we get down three or four points."

One reason McMahon had been upset about missing the game was he never had played on national TV. He missed the 1984 playoffs because of his kidney injury. "Not too many peo-ple know about Jim McMahon," he said.

They did now. Not only did he throw three touchdown passes in 6 minutes and 59 seconds, he improvised on all three of them. The Vikings blitzed on that first play, the 70-yard pass to Willie Gault. McMahon was hit as he threw the ball. But Gault, who changed his pass route, caught the ball at the Vikings' 30.

McMahon threw the second pass, to Dennis McKinnon, running to his left away from the rush. McKinnon caught the third touchdown, too, after the primary receiver was covered.

When McMahon first came to the huddle, the other Bears were shocked not to see Steve Fuller, who had started. McMahon greeted them by cussing them out. Then he said, "We're going to go down that field and get six."

McMahon completed 8 of 15 for 236 yards. Gault's 146 yards, on six catches, was a career high. McKinnon had four catches, for 133 yards.

"It wasn't just one guy," Payton said. "It was Dennis and Willie making catches, the offensive line sucking it up and blocking. It's wonderful a machine like this can work together."

The defense forced five turnovers, too. But let's not get carried away with the team picture. This game was McMahon's.

"The last couple years," coach Mike Ditka said, "everything we've done has been with a sledgehammer. Bam! Bam! Bam! And there's a lot of room for error when you do it that way. Now we can get points fast, too."

Anything you can do, we can do better, the Bears were saying. Anything. Before the game, Vikings coach Bud Grant had caused a stir by challenging ABC to televise the National Anthem because his players lined up so smartly at attention. Then, when the Anthem started, the Bears slapped their right hands over their hearts in unison. The Vikings didn't. "I don't ever want to be upstaged in anything in life," Ditka said.

It took an extraordinary relief performance by quarterback Jim McMahon (right) in a nationally televised Thursday night game to keep the Bears unbeaten. Idled by a back injury, McMahon entered the game midway through the third quarter with the Vikings leading 17-9.

On his first play, McMahon (left) rolled right and found wide receiver Willie Gault open for a 70-yard touchdown (below). The quarterback celebrated the score by butting heads with wide receiver Ken Margerum (below right). By the time the period ended, McMahon had thrown two more touchdown passes and Chicago was on its way to a 33-24 victory.

The Chargers and Bengals put on a spectacular show in Cincinnati, combining for 965 yards. San Diego quarterback Dan Fouts (right), protected by 17-year veteran Ed White, completed 25 of 43 passes for 344 yards and four touchdowns in the Chargers' 44-41 victory. By season's end, White had set an all-time NFL record for most games by an offensive lineman—241.

Chargers '85

The lightning was back in the Chargers' offense. They trailed 41-34 at Cincinnati when quarterback Dan Fouts uncorked the old *Zap!* His 60-yard touchdown pass to Lionel (Little Train) James tied the score with four minutes left. When Fouts got the ball back on a fumble, he drove San Diego to its 44-41 victory.

James was the season's most exciting offensive discovery. The 5-foot 6-inch running back led the AFC with 86 catches. He set NFL records with 1,027 yards receiving by a back and 2,535 combined yards on runs, receptions, and returns.

The most exciting offensive resurrection was Fouts's passing arm. Injuries had slowed him the previous two years, and the Chargers had ground to a near standstill in the nine games he missed. Now he was back in the Pro Bowl with 27 touchdown passes and a league-high 8.46 yards per attempt. When gimpy knees kept him out of two games and parts of several others, reserve Mark Herrmann merely led the league in passing. The Chargers' 304 passing yards a game led the NFL. They also led the league in total offense and scoring.

The Chargers finished 8-8 after two losing seasons. They started at 3-5, then beat both AFC West leaders, the Broncos and the Raiders. Their offense sparkled with the addition of USFL refugees Tim Spencer and Gary Anderson in the backfield and rookie tackle Jim Lachey. Charlie Joiner, 38, added 59 catches to his all-time NFL record total (now 716).

But oh, that defense. It ranked last again and got coordinator Tom Bass fired early and sent his successor, Dave Adolph, back to Cleveland later. Still, it had some promising youngsters.

Week 4

Bears 45, Redskins 10

The Bears had become as desperate to prove points as they were to score them. They were one of only two 3-0 teams in the NFL, but people still thought of them as the same old, plodding Bears. Here they had gone to the trouble of a major facelift, and they still were getting no respect.

Defenses kept on stacking eight men at the line to stop their running game, daring them to pass. They hadn't seemed to notice the Bears' comebacks from 14 and 9 points behind, not even the previous week's shootout at Minnesota. The hometown fans weren't exactly brimming with faith, either. When Washington jumped ahead 10-0, coach Mike Ditka said, "There were a couple of curse words going through the crowd." A few boos, too.

There was only one solution: A good, old-fashioned trouncing of a well-regarded team would chase those gremlins from the Bears' closet once and for all. The unfortunate Redskins got in the way and took a 45-10 beating, their worst since 1961. The 31-point second quarter was a Chicago record.

The Bears did it with two offensive linemen and a defensive back injured and missing. They did it with Walter Payton running seven times for six yards, his third-poorest total since he was a rookie. They did it with their first disadvantage in possession time since 1983. They did it with their fewest rushing yards, passing yards, and first downs of the season.

"We didn't do anything offensively except capitalize on what the defense gave us," Ditka said. That's enough. That's what championship teams do. They make big plays and turn them into points. The Bears spun 38 of their points out of 6:54 in possession time. They used to take that long to produce a field goal.

Championship teams don't get down on themselves when they fall behind in the early stages of a game. The Redskins outgained the Bears

141-2 in the first quarter, recalling defensive coordinator Buddy Ryan's condemnation of "our Swiss cheese defense—they've got holes in them and they stink." Quarterback Jim McMahon was 0 for 4 with an interception. "We needed a spark," he said.

It came from Willie Gault. His 99-yard kickoff return ignited a 28-point explosion in 10:25. Gault almost didn't make it through the first hole at the 20-yard line, but Dennis Gentry and Shaun Gayle turned him loose with blocks. The world-class sprinter juked and dashed past the last two Redskins on the right sideline, and it was a 10-7 game.

"He was the catalyst," Ditka said. "He was a catalyst last week, too [against the Vikings]. You've seen not only what Willie means to this team, but the impact he's going to have on our league. His speed is just exceptional. I marvel at what he does."

The Redskins' next three possessions netted a total of one yard. With punter Jeff Hayes injured, Joe Theismann shanked a one-yard punt and lost a fumble. The Bears responded with touchdown drives of 14, 22, and 36 yards. McMahon threw for the first two touchdowns and caught a pass from Payton for the third.

The other two touchdowns were plays that McMahon changed from runs to passes at the line of scrimmage. No longer did the Bears have to grit their teeth and run into eight-man fronts. Payton told McMahon on the sideline, "If you see the blitz, just keep throwing the ball."

It was only the third time in 11 years the Bears won with Payton gaining less than 40 yards. They broke Washington's 22-game winning streak in games in which it scored first. They won their third game of the season after trailing by more than a touchdown, something they had done only twice in 44 previous games. They led the league in scoring. They were off to their best start since the 1963 championship season.

When quarterback Jim McMahon (right) caught a 13-yard scoring pass from Walter Payton, it capped a four-touchdown outburst in the second quarter and helped the Bears to a commanding 31-10 halftime lead over Washington.

Things went from bad to worse for the Redskins when quarterback Joe Theismann (right), substituting for injured punter Jeff Hayes, shanked a one-yard punt to set up another Chicago score. John Riggins (far right) was held to 29 yards rushing by Wilber Marshall (58) and an angry Bears defense. Final score: Bears 45, Redskins 10.

Rookie quarterback Randall Cunningham of Philadelphia (right) was uprooted by Giants linebacker Lawrence Taylor. Eventually, Cunningham left the game with an injured ankle, and New York left with a 16-10 overtime victory.

Giants '85

Piece by piece, the New York Giants appear to be putting together a champion. In 1985, they added a running game. Joe Morris, 5-7 and 195 pounds, finally gave them the ball control to complement their fearsome defense. He led the league with 21 rushing touchdowns and ranked fourth with 1,336 yards, a team record. The Giants vaulted from twenty-second to fourth in the rushing rankings.

Phil Simms had a Pro Bowl year at quarterback, too, but the Giants' best games were when he passed the least. They wore opponents out with the one-two punch of running and defense, just as they did against Philadelphia in the 16-10 overtime victory that kept them tied for first place with a 3-1 record.

They lost a 10-3 lead on an interception return with 3:02 left. But Elvis Patterson's 29-yard interception return won the game on the second play of overtime.

Patterson was replacing holdout cornerback Mark Haynes surprisingly well. He had been burned so often in 1984, he was nicknamed Toast. Haynes never did get his job back after signing. The Giants' five Pro Bowl players were their most since 1963. They were the only top-10 team in all six offensive and defensive rankings.

"This is a young team, a growing team with a collection of some of the best athletes in the game," coach Bill Parcells said. The only obvious piece still missing was the intangible to win big games and close games. Their 10-6 record earned only a wild-card bid.

Great as the defense was, it blew fourth-quarter leads in four defeats. It ranked second to the Bears in total and rushing yards, and led the league with 68 sacks.

Week 5

Bears 27, Buccaneers 19

It was the kind of game winning teams win and losing teams lose. At halftime at Tampa Stadium, even after the Bears' late field goal, underdog Tampa Bay led 12-3. "We felt we had complete control of the game," Buccaneers tight end Jimmie Giles said.

When it ended 27-19 for the 5-0 Bears instead of for the 0-5 Bucs, the Bears understood how Tampa Bay felt. They had been on the wrong side of more near-upsets than their veterans cared to remember. They had sat in locker rooms shaking their heads, marveling at how lucky those Vikings or Cowboys or Raiders were to escape with a victory. They had wondered how those teams won games they should have lost. Now they knew.

"The thing that sets this team apart," said Walter Payton, "is, regardless of how far behind we get or how many mistakes we make, nobody loses confidence in the system or the people."

The Bears had chances to give in right up to the final 5:21 when a Tampa Bay touchdown cut their lead to 20-19. There were four minutes left when quarterback Jim McMahon and coach Mike Ditka talked about what to do on third-and-three from the Bears' 24. Plenty of time for the Buccaneers to drive for the winning field goal. Still, the safe choice would have been to try a running play, and, if it didn't work, let the defense save the game.

That's what Ditka wanted to do when McMahon reached the sideline. McMahon argued. He wanted to throw a slant-out to Emery Moorehead, whose seven catches for 106 yards already was the best game for a Bears tight end since Ditka was playing. Ditka gave in. Moorehead caught the pass for an 8-yard gain.

Three plays later, the coach and quarterback visited again at the two-minute warning. The Bears had made another first down. It was second-and-11 at their 41. Even more tempting to play it safe.

McMahon would have none of it. He was sure the Bucs would blitz. They had to force the action. It was a perfect time for a long pass over the middle to Willie Gault.

"I just know that when I try to play it close to the vest, that's when we don't play good football," Ditka said. "When I let Jim wheel and deal back there and give him a lot of leeway, he plays better. He thrives on it."

So Ditka approved that long pass, and Gault caught it with a tumble at the Buccaneers' 11-yard line. Two plays later, Payton's second touchdown run of the day clinched the game.

Confidence. That's the downhill slope in the snowball effect of winning. After four consecutive victories, the Bears' confidence had approached the point of sneering contempt for the poor suckers who had to play them. The Wednesday before the Tampa Bay game, linebacker Otis Wilson had started in on the standard spiel of how the Buccaneers were a tough team and would pose a challenge. Then he remembered they were winless and said, "So it shouldn't be too much of a challenge."

"We're relaxed," safety Gary Fencik said. "We're able to take chances. If something doesn't work, it's not the end of the world. But when you're relaxed, it's going to work more times than it doesn't."

It worked in the third quarter when Dave Duerson broke for the ball a step sooner than Giles and intercepted it. Six plays later, with a cornerback covering him like suntan lotion, Dennis McKinnon caught the touchdown pass that cut the deficit to 12-10.

Three more plays later, the Bears' alignment worried quarterback Steve DeBerg about a blitz. He pulled out before he had the snap. Steve McMichael saw it before the center. He fell on the ball. The Bears were in position for their go-ahead field goal. Another lucky break? In the NFL, luck is an acquired skill.

Play it again, Jim. As in week 1, Tampa Bay took an early lead over the Bears and expanded it by halftime. Following the same script, Jim McMahon (right) got hot and led a second-half comeback as Chicago rallied for a 27-19 victory. Walter Payton ran for two touchdowns, becoming the sixth player in NFL history to score 100 career touchdowns.

There was no lack of excitement in Cleveland in week 5 when local hero Bernie Kosar made his NFL debut at quarterback for the Browns. New England took a 20-17 lead in the third quarter as Cleveland cornerback Frank Minnifield and Patriots wide receiver Stanley Morgan choreographed their version of a football pas de deux. As the play unfolded in the Browns' end zone (below), Minnifield blocked Morgan's vision with his left arm (1) and

appeared to be in good position for a possible interception (2). With the ball up for grabs (3), the two combatants maintained remarkable concentration (4) as the duel continued. Even though Al Gross arrived to assist Minnifield (5), Morgan began to close in on the ball, and he held on for a 22-yard touchdown while falling to the turf (6). But Kosar rallied the Browns to a 24-20 victory, enabling him to walk off the field (right) a winner.

Browns '85

When the Browns lost their opener in overtime, coach Marty Schottenheimer said, "Don't anybody think for a minute this is 1984 revisited." That 5-11 Cleveland team had lost nine games in the last two minutes. Now, four weeks later in their next nail-biter, the Browns stopped New England on fourth down, six inches from the goal line, with four minutes left. It preserved the 24-20 victory that put them in first place in the AFC Central with a 3-2 record.

It was the first NFL game for Bernie Kosar, the blue-chip rookie quarterback the Browns had obtained through the supplementary draft for two first-round picks. When Gary Danielson hurt his shoulder trying to tackle the Patriot who intercepted his second-quarter pass, Kosar's apprenticeship ended. He guided the Browns to their winning touchdown with 12:12 to play.

Danielson never fully recovered. Kosar had his ups and downs. The Browns were 4-6 after losing four in a row, including two one-pointers in the closing seconds. But they won four of their next five. Their 8-8 record hardly was imposing, but was enough to win the AFC Central.

Fortunately, Kosar had a strong defense and running game to lean on. The running game was something new. It had ranked twenty-first in 1984, but former USFL player Kevin Mack's 115 yards against New England lifted the Browns to second. They finished eighth with the third 1,000-yard tandem in NFL history— 1,104 for Mack and 1,002 for Earnest Byner.

It was Kosar who carried the Browns over the top in week 15, when their 28-21 victory over Houston virtually clinched the division. He ran for one touchdown and passed for three.

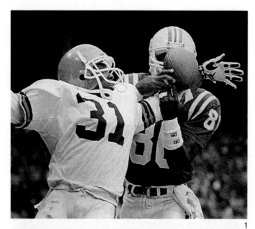
1

2

3

4

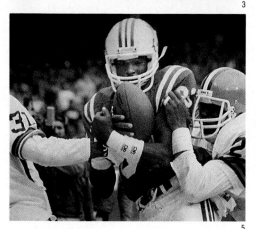
5

6

Redskins '85

The Redskins climbed out of the grave, but they stayed on the ground. That's where they're best. They manhandled St. Louis 27-10 in a Monday night game with John Riggins running 17 times for 103 yards and George Rogers 25 for 104.

Washington's 45-10 drubbing in Chicago had left it in last place at 1-3, ranked twenty-fifth in passing and tied for twenty-sixth in scoring. The aging Redskins' obituary was written even before the season. Their heir-apparent was St. Louis, which won three of its first four. Who could imagine on October 7 that Washington would wind up 10-6 and St. Louis 5-11?

The transition from old to young was orderly. Rogers gradually replaced Riggins as the main ball carrier. His Redskins' record 206 yards in the last game gave him 1,093 for the season, a 4.7 average. Washington was second in NFL rushing.

At quarterback, things changed more abruptly. Joe Theismann's leg was shattered in week 11, again on Monday night. The Redskins were 5-5 with the NFL's fewest passing yards when Jay Schroeder came off the bench. They came back to beat the Giants 23-21, then won their last three for the sixth consecutive year.

The third-ranked defense led the league against the pass with three rookies in the Nickel lineup. Ends Dexter Manley and Charles Mann ranked fourth and fifth in NFL sacks.

Schroeder hadn't played as a 1984 rookie. He was drafted in the third round, but he had turned to baseball after his second season at UCLA, 1980. Could he do it? Any doubts evaporated during weeks 14 and 15. He overcame injuries and leads to win twice: 17-12 after Philadelphia led 12-3, and 27-24 after Cincinnati led 24-7.

The Washington Redskins ground out a 27-10 victory over visiting St. Louis on a Monday night, as George Rogers (left) ran for 104 yards on 25 carries and John Riggins added 103 on 17. It marked the first time two Redskins ever had rushed for 100 yards in the same game. A case could be made for the defense, too, with its five interceptions, including one by linebacker Rich Milot (below).

Week 6

Bears 26, 49ers 10

San Francisco had been the last team to beat the Bears. "I thought about that game a lot when I was lifting weights in the offseason," center Jay Hilgenberg said. Coach Mike Ditka did, too. The 49ers had exposed the flaw in the Bears' run-oriented offense of 1984. They had embarrassed the Bears 23-0 in the NFC Championship Game. A national magazine had praised the Bears' defense but said, "Next time, bring an offense." That became their rallying cry long before they found their Candlestick Park locker room wallpapered with clippings from the 23-0 game.

"We remembered to pack an offense," tackle Jimbo Covert said after the Bears returned to that locker room.

The Bears absolutely toyed with the Super Bowl champs. They won much more convincingly than the 26-10 score. They shut down the vaunted San Francisco offense like a bad restaurant. They jumped out to a 16-0 lead, let the game grow tantalizingly close, and then unleashed Walter Payton to crush them into the ground as though they were a cigarette butt.

Ditka said he hoped it was another giant step, like the one the Bears took when they beat the defending champion Raiders in 1984. "You have to use the world champions as a barometer," he said. "We beat the best."

But did they? Or did they *replace* the best? They had trounced two other defending division champions and had taken a three-game lead in their own division. They were 6-0 for the first time since 1942.

The offense called passes on 15 of its first 20 plays. Even with flanker Dennis McKinnon and tight end Emery Moorehead out, the Bears passed for 115 yards in the first quarter and scored the first four times they had the ball.

"I made up my mind I was not going to come out and play it the way I did last time," Ditka said. "I told the players, we're not going to go run-run-run-and-punt again. We were going to make them fear something. We went out and challenged them."

The defense set up the third and fourth scores by forcing fumbles. Then, after Carlton Williamson's 43-yard interception return for a 49ers touchdown and a late first-half field goal gave San Francisco hope, the defense took over to protect a lead that stayed at six points.

The 49ers had three first downs and 45 yards in the second half. They finished with 11 first downs and 183 yards, all-time lows for the seven-year regime of coach Bill Walsh. They got just 67 yards rushing.

Joe Montana is at his best when he gets rid of the ball within two seconds. But when corner-backs Mike Richardson and Leslie Frazier jammed his receivers at the line, he had to wait longer. With defensive tackles Dan Hampton and Steve McMichael in his face, he couldn't step up from the rush, as he does so well. Montana's seven sacks were a career high.

"When you get a lead, you get a pass rush," said McMichael, who reduced Pro Bowl guard Randy Cross to a journeyman on this day.

But Montana still had time to pull the game out after rookie Kevin Butler's fourth field goal made it 19-10 and the Bears got the ball back with 11:41 left. That was when, as Payton said, "We tried to do something a little bit different."

What Bears fan ever thought he would live to hear giving Payton the ball called "something different"? Payton carried nine times on a 13-play drive. He gained 52 of the 66 yards, and carried two defenders the last three yards on his 17-yard touchdown run with 3:41 left. His 24 carries and 132 yards were season highs.

"I don't care how well McMahon plays," Hampton said, "Payton's still the heart and soul of that offense." The Bears hadn't needed him much so far, but they were glad to see he could still turn on the old magic.

The Showdown by the Bay became a Blow-out by the Bay. Bears wide receiver Willie Gault (right) turned on the speed and left San Francisco's Tory Nixon at his heels.

The swarming Chicago defense stripped the ball from Wendell Tyler (26, left) on a day when the 49ers could gain only 67 yards rushing. ''Old Bear football,'' said coach Mike Ditka (above) of his team's impressive 26-10 victory.

Dallas had not beaten the Steelers since 1972...until week 6 in 1985. Cowboys placekicker Rafael Septien (below) kicked two field goals to extend his scoring streak to 124 consecutive games. But the day belonged to Tony Dorsett (right), who grew up in the Pittsburgh suburb of Aliquippa. Dorsett ran for 113 yards in the Cowboys' 27-13 victory, becoming only the sixth player in NFL history to rush for more than 10,000 yards.

Cowboys '85

The Cowboys found themselves in the unusual role of Cinderella team, a notion they encouraged by losing 44-0 to Chicago and 50-24 to Cincinnati. They were nobody else's patsies, though. They bounced back from Cincinnati to beat the Giants 28-21, clinching their first division title in four years.

Many had picked Dallas to finish fourth, and coach Tom Landry agreed that made sense. The offense had finished the 1984 season without a running game. The defense was mostly enthusiastic kids who could play over their heads, but not always.

Dallas wore its vulnerability well. It was no longer a plastic team. The youngsters pumped life into the team, and Landry obviously loved it. He warned them that they couldn't forget that emotion or they would "lose to just about anybody."

When Dallas beat Pittsburgh for the first time in six tries, 27-13, coach Chuck Noll said, "It looked like the Cowboys' defense of old. They put pressure on us up front, and we couldn't handle it." Steelers quarterbacks completed only 13 of 40 passes, with three interceptions. That gave the 5-1 Cowboys 18 interceptions. They finished the season with 33, one behind the league-leading Bears.

The Cowboys no longer were above such "gimmicks" as blitzing, which they did as much as anybody. Their defense ranked fourth with 62 sacks, including Ed Jones's career-high 13 and Jim Jeffcoat's 12.

Tony Dorsett was a threat again, ranking sixth with 1,307 yards rushing, his eighth 1,000-yard season. He broke the 10,000-yard milestone against his boyhood idols, helping to beat the Steelers with a 56-yard touchdown catch and a 35-yard run.

Week 7

Bears 23, Packers 7

All week, Chicagoans were buzzing over the "Twilight Zone" ending coach Mike Ditka had given the San Francisco game. On the last two plays, the Bears' ball carrier was rookie defensive tackle William (The Refrigerator) Perry. He was more back-and-a-half than running back, even though his weight had slipped from 330 pounds to 308 since training camp. But he gained two yards each time. The signoff on TV fairly begged for a "To Be Continued."

What began as a twist of the knife — payback for the 49ers using guard Guy McIntyre as a blocking back late in the 1984 NFC Championship Game — turned into a twist of fate. Ditka was joking when he said during the week he was planning a flea-flicker to Perry. But he was as serious as an undertaker when he said, "Gives you a little food for thought on the goal line, doesn't he?"

Food? That was the only word Perry needed to hear. In his encore performance against Green Bay at Soldier Field, The Refrigerator ran for one short touchdown and blocked spectacularly for two more. He got the offensive game ball for the 23-7 victory, and his one-yard run took him to the end of the rainbow. It just so happened to be a Monday night game. The world watched with wide eyes and belly laughs. Perry's plays were shown over and over again from Laramie to London. From Ditka's fertile imagination and Perry's rural charm, a legend was hatched.

"I was just having fun," Perry said, the chorus he would dance to all season.

"We'll probably keep putting him in there until they can put somebody bigger in who can plug up the hole," Ditka said.

"It was great to have him back there because he's great to hide behind," said Walter Payton, who scored from the 2 and the 1. "No one can see you back there."

Perry's first offensive appearance was earth-shaking, literally and figuratively. Early in the second quarter, the Bears trailed 7-0 but had first-and-goal at the 2. Perry lined up behind the right tackle, with Payton behind the quarterback. Perry met 224-pound linebacker George Cumby in the hole and bent him backward like a fiberglass pole. "You murdelized him," Perry's teammates told him after Payton scored easily.

"I think I rung his bell," Perry said of the splat heard 'round the world.

Four minutes later, the Bears had first-and-goal at the 1. Quarterback Jim McMahon led the Soldier Field cheers as Perry lumbered in. This time, he was his own lead blocker. "I think I was stepping on people when I went in," Perry said of his touchdown. After taking a few seconds to untangle himself, Perry spiked the ball hard enough to leave a sizable dent.

What was Perry's running style? "No style," he said. "Just straight ahead."

Late in the first half, one more time, first-and-goal inside the 1. "Per-ree! Per-ree!" chanted the crowd. Ditka milked it, sending in two other substitutes, then looking down and beckoning The Refrigerator as though he'd almost forgotten. The crowd grew louder.

Perry lined up on the left, but the play was the same as the first. "It was like stealing. I just walked into the end zone," Payton said.

"He tried to look at me," Perry said of Cumby. "I believe he was looking at stars."

"Both plays were awesome," Ditka said. "Usually when two bodies hit, there's an impact point and both bodies stop a little bit. But they hit and it was like an earth mover. He just moved it out."

There was method to Ditka's madness. Before this game, the Bears had scored touchdowns on only 6 of 10 drives after crossing the 5 with goal to go. Now they were 9 for 13.

Under Perry's considerable shadow, the rest of the game seemed like sideshow acts.

Walter Payton (right) continued his personal assault on record books as he rushed for 112 yards and two touchdowns to become the Bears' all-time leading scorer with 630 points. The biggest cheers of the evening, however, were reserved for a rotund rookie named William (The Refrigerator) Perry, who cleared the way for Payton's touchdowns and scored one himself in the 23-7 victory over Green Bay.

Rams '85

Maybe it was time to take the Los Angeles Rams seriously after all. Seven games and they still were undefeated, just like the Bears. But something was missing. That flair. Where the Bears came on like marauding hordes, the Rams reminded people of pickpockets.

They put eight men in pass coverage, not on the line of scrimmage. Their defense didn't force mistakes as much as it coaxed them. It worked, though. When Todd Blackledge replaced injured Bill Kenney at Kansas City, the Rams intercepted him six times and won 16-0. LeRoy Irvin had two for the second-consecutive game. The Rams wound up third behind the Bears and Cowboys in takeaways, with 29 interceptions and 17 fumbles.

If people didn't take them seriously, it was because they seemed so lucky. They finished with the NFL's fewest passing yards. Fourteen teams outscored them.

The Rams' success was all the more remarkable considering their offense. Quarterback Dieter Brock was new from Canada. Deep threat Ron Brown was injured early. Eric Dickerson rarely got untracked after his two-game holdout. His 1,234 yards were good, but hardly Dickersonian, until he drove Dallas from the playoffs with 248.

The defense corrected its only weakness. Linebacker Mike Wilcher and rejuvenated end Gary Jeter led the charge to 56 sacks. And the kicking teams were sensational, with league-leading net punter Dale Hatcher, punt returner Henry Ellard, and kickoff returner Brown, who had three touchdowns.

Their 11-5 record, three years after they finished at 2-7, gave the Rams their first Western Division championship since 1979.

Eagles '85

Ron Jaworski knew what to do when Dallas blitzed nine men. "Get rid of the ball," said Philadelphia's quarterback. There was a place for an old guy behind the center after all. Jaworski unloaded the ball to Kenny Jackson, who went untouched for the 36-yard touchdown that upset the Cowboys 16-14.

Suddenly, the Eagles were 3-4, only two games behind division-leading Dallas. Two weeks earlier, they had been 1-4. Jaworski was replaced by rookie Randall Cunningham after taking eight sacks in the opener. But he was back for game 6. His three touchdown passes beat St. Louis 30-7. Now he ripped the Cowboys' league-leading pass defense for 380 yards.

The Eagles looked genuine when they climbed to 6-5, with a chance to catch the Cowboys the next week. Earnest Jackson was on his way to Philadelphia's first 1,000-yard rushing season since 1981. Reggie White, who arrived from the USFL after four games, would tie Greg Brown for the team lead with 13 sacks. Mike Quick had another Pro Bowl year. He led NFC receivers with 1,247 yards and 11 touchdowns, including a 99-yard play that beat Atlanta in overtime.

Then things fell apart. The rematch against Dallas started a four-game losing streak. New owner Norman Braman criticized coach Marion Campbell's defense.

The players couldn't save Campbell's job. He was gone before the last game. The players taped "Fox 78" to their uniforms that final Sunday, honoring Campbell's Swamp Fox nickname and old Eagles uniform number. They won. Two days after Super Bowl XX, their new coach was Buddy Ryan, the Bears' defensive coordinator.

Dallas had its four-game winning streak snapped when the Eagles' Ron Jaworski (below) threw for a career-high 380 yards in a 16-14 victory. Wide receiver Kenny Jackson scored the go-ahead points in the fourth quarter when he caught a 36-yard pass from Jaworski that first was tipped by cornerback Everson Walls. A major part of the Philadelphia story was defense, as defensive end Reggie White demonstrated by sacking Cowboys quarterback Gary Hogeboom (right).

Week 8

Bears 27, Vikings 9

The Bears' defense had changed more subtly than their offense. It didn't have as much room for improvement. The year before, it had led the league in yards, rushing yards, first downs, fewest points allowed, third-down efficiency, and pass-completion percentage. But what's this? Tied for tenth in interceptions? Disgraceful.

"The guys get it in our minds that we can knock the receiver out," linebacker Mike Singletary said. "But do we want to do that or do we want the ball? It was a decision we had to make, which one would be more effective."

It helped that they used zone coverage a little more often. They already had been forcing the hurried throws that go off-target, and now the backs and linebackers were looking for the ball. After the host Bears made five interceptions in beating Minnesota 27-9, their 21 through eight games equaled their 16-game total for 1984. Midway through the season, they were the only undefeated team and were leading the league both in points scored and fewest points allowed.

Two interceptions decided the game in the third quarter. Otis Wilson returned one 23 yards for the touchdown that made the score 20-7. Wilber Marshall grabbed one at the Bears' 3-yard line to keep the score 20-7.

"They put a lot of pressure on you and create turnovers," Vikings quarterback Tommy Kramer said. "They have outstanding people. Their scheme is working because they have the personnel to do it."

Those people have the instinct for the ball. On Wilson's interception, defensive end Richard Dent got to Kramer just as he started throwing. It was too late for a sack, so Dent grabbed the quarterback's arm from behind. The wobbling ball bounced off defensive tackle Steve Mc-Michael and straight to Wilson.

Three minutes later, the Vikings were at the Bears' 1-yard line, second-and-goal. Darrin Nelson angled from the backfield to the right

pylon, looking for a pass, but the rush made Kramer throw the ball early.

Marshall picked it off just before it reached Nelson. He had two for the game and four for the season. "They pick on me because I'm a rookie," Marshall said, overlooking his 1984 season on the bench.

The real rookie, William Perry, tried defensive tackle on for size this time. "That's what I've been wanting to do," he said. "I came here to sack quarterbacks, not score touchdowns." He liked his first NFL sack better than his touchdown the week before. He didn't have any goal-line opportunities on offense, but played most of the game on defense for the first time and earned his way into the starting lineup for the last eight games.

"We'll use the reverse to him next week," coach Mike Ditka said. And then the option pass? "As soon as he jumps over the goal post."

The Bears didn't need him to pass, even though Jim McMahon's lower back was in such pain that he missed much of the fourth quarter for the second straight game. That didn't keep Chicago from passing on 13 of 19 first downs. And Walter Payton's third straight 100-yard game gave him 362 yards in the last three games, 72 more than he had in the first five.

They led 7-0 after three-and-a-half minutes. McMahon's touchdown pass to Dennis McKinnon went 33 yards. It was an audible, of course. McKinnon had seven touchdown catches—tops in the NFC—and six of them were on audibles or broken plays.

He was McMahon's old reliable, a receiver who could get open on third-and-eight, fight for the underthrown ball, or leave a defender grasping for air after a fancy fake. Not to mention "block like a guard," as former Bears tight end Jay Saldi had said. In two-and-a-half seasons, the Bears were 13-0 in games in which Mc-Kinnon scored a touchdown.

High-flying Walter Payton (right) ran for 118 yards and caught a 20-yard scoring pass from Jim McMahon as the Bears defeated Minnesota 27-9. Chicago's monsters were a perfect 8-0 at the midway.

Lions '85

Going to the Lions' noisy Silver-dome was like a trip to the principal's office. Dallas couldn't get out without a licking. Neither could San Francisco. Now Miami was rubbing away a 31-21 sting. In consecutive weeks, Detroit had upset both of the previous year's Super Bowl teams.

How were they doing it? Mirrors? "It's hard to pinpoint something that we're doing," coach Darryl Rogers said. "If we could, we would have done it sooner. Our offense hasn't had any spectacular days."

The Miami game wasn't bad. James Jones, picking up the slack for the missing Billy Sims, ran for 100 yards. Eric Hipple passed for three touchdowns. The defense shut Dan Marino down by sagging into deep zones.

"I don't think these games put us in a class where people will be shaking in their boots to play us," Rogers said. If anything, Rogers's success was not making the *Lions* shake in their boots. He was so easygoing, people called the team Mr. Rogers's Neighborhood. Players welcomed the change.

The rest of the season went downhill, from 5-3 to 7-9. The Lions upset the Jets at home on Thanksgiving Day, but lost their last two, at home, to Green Bay and Chicago. And they won only once on the road, where the Colts and Buccaneers beat them.

The amazing thing was that they'd gone 5-3 in the first place. They were coming off a 4-11-1 season. They had a new head coach from the colleges and a staff with hardly any pro experience. Their best player, Sims, missed the entire season with a knee injury. His replacement, Wilbert Montgomery, was a shadow of himself before missing the last eight games. Injuries ravaged the offensive linemen and linebackers.

It was another super Sunday in Detroit as Eric Hipple (below) completed 14 of 19 passes for 239 yards to lead the NFL's giant-killers, the Lions, past Miami 31-21. Just a week earlier at the Silverdome, Detroit had surprised San Francisco, the other Super Bowl XIX participant, 23-21. Linebacker Roosevelt Barnes (right) clinched the victory when he intercepted a Dan Marino pass with 1:27 left to play.

And then there was one. . . . With versatile running back Roger Craig leading the way, San Francisco jumped to a 28-0 halftime lead over the Rams. The 49ers coasted to a 28-14 victory, leaving Chicago as the NFL's only unbeaten team. Craig, who scored twice, finished the 49ers' scoring late in the first half when he caught a rollout jump pass from quarterback Joe Montana and beat safety Johnnie Johnson (20) in a footrace down the sideline (right) for a 35-yard touchdown.

49ers '85

Nobody considered the 49ers a 3-4 team. Technically, yes, they had won three and lost four. But they were always a smoldering fire. The Bears thrashed them in week 6, then kept glancing at them over their shoulders until the Giants knocked them out of the playoffs.

Everything seemed back to normal when San Francisco beat the Rams 28-14 in week 8. The 49ers appeared to had gotten losing out of their system.

"It's clear we were overwhelmed by them," Rams coach John Robinson said after 49ers quarterback Joe Montana threw three touchdown passes in the 28-0 first half. From there, San Francisco won 4 of 5 while the Rams lost 3 of 5, and the Rams' early four-game lead had shrunk to one when they played again in week 14. But the Rams won the rematch. The 49ers had to win their last two games to go 10-6.

Their problems went beyond the snowball in Denver, which bolixed a field-goal attempt in their only loss in a six-game stretch. As coach Bill Walsh said after the 26-10 loss to the Bears, they were playing like "a very average football team." Fred Dean, good for a sack a game in previous seasons, had three all year. The 49ers gave up 42 sacks, up 15 from 1984.

Many parts of the 49ers' game were spectacular, but too seldom at the same time. Montana's 27 touchdowns and 91.3 rating led NFC passers. Rookie Jerry Rice overcame early drops to gain 927 yards on 49 catches (including a team-record 241-yard game in the loss to the Rams.) Roger Craig led the NFL with 92 catches and was the first player to clear 1,000 yards both running and receiving. Only the Bears allowed fewer points.

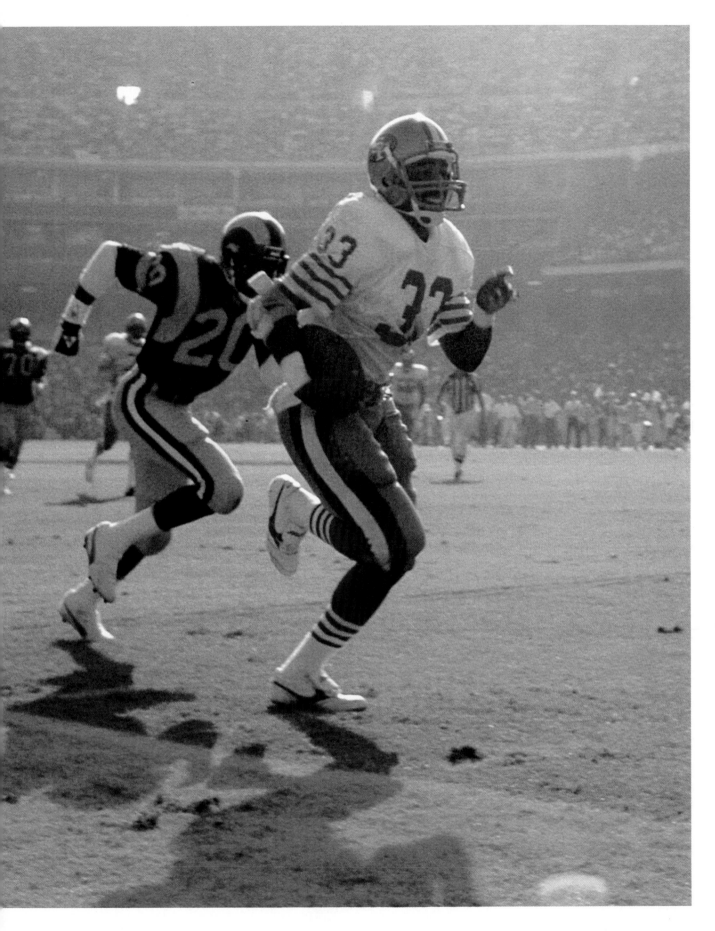

W e e k   9

Bears 16, Packers 10

On the second play, Packers safety Ken Stills slugged Bears quarterback Jim McMahon in a pileup when the ball was dead. On the ninth play, Packers cornerback Mark Lee crashed Walter Payton into the wall like a hockey player, knocking over the Bears' bench on the way. Later in the first quarter, Stills leveled running back Matt Suhey well after the whistle. Lee was ejected. Stills was penalized and fined $500. The first quarter had 97 yards in penalties. The first half had six personal fouls.

"This was like World War III without nuclear weapons," Bears coach Mike Ditka said. He also called the 16-10 victory "by far our toughest game." It was the Bears' sixth comeback victory, but their first by less than a touchdown and the first time they trailed in the fourth quarter. If they could win that one, Dan Hampton said, they could go undefeated.

"We played up there. We played horrible. They played the best they've ever played against us," Suhey recalled a few weeks later. "They used all kinds of fighting, cheap shots. And they still didn't beat us."

The teams had sent threatening messages across the state line all week. The Packers vowed revenge for the double-team block that injured quarterback Lynn Dickey 20 or 30 yards from a pass interception in the first meeting. Aside from Dickey, who did not play, Hampton said, "I wouldn't give you two cents for the whole Green Bay Packers team." Packers tackle Greg Koch responded, "He must be giving a penny a sack."

"They don't like us and we don't like them," Ditka said. "That's the way football is supposed to be played."

The Bears were greeted in their locker room by a five-pound bag of fertilizer, courtesy of a Milwaukee radio station. "Here's what you guys are full of," the note said.

But suddenly, in the second half, football

broke out. Payton turned the focus from broken rules to the broken field. He passed the 14,000-yard milestone at a blur and finished with 28 carries for 192 yards, his most since 1977. With 10:31 to play, he broke a tackle five yards downfield and scored the 27-yard touchdown that put the Bears ahead 16-10.

"Everybody should have taken their face-masks off and put on black high-tops," Steve Mc-Michael said.

"It was just nasty," Mike Singletary said, smiling. "Our kind of football. We enjoyed that."

What could the Packers have been thinking? Clobbering and jabbering like they were, they only got Payton riled. "That doesn't intimidate me. It just motivates me," he said.

Even William Perry couldn't upstage Payton. Even by giving new meaning to the term wide receiver. Even by catching McMahon's four-yard touchdown pass without breaking stride. It gave the Bears a 7-3 lead 25 seconds before halftime.

Perry lined up at left wingback and went in motion. When he got to the corner, the linebacker who met him was George Cumby. Remember him? Cumby braced for Perry's block and Perry ran around him.

The amazing thing was that the players had to wait after the huddle for the wildly pro-Packers crowd at Lambeau Field to quiet down. The Bears knew what was coming and no one giggled. "The only thing I was upset about," Jay Hilgenberg said, "was he said he was going to do a 360 dunk over the goal post."

It was Perry's second go-ahead touchdown against Green Bay in 13 days. When Packers coach Forrest Gregg thought about it, his face melted into a smile. "He was beautiful, wasn't he?" Gregg said. "He's a heck of an athlete."

But he's no Payton. "I've been a Bear fan all my life," Dave Duerson said. "And I think Walter's reaching his peak."

"I hope he's right," Payton said.

Walter Payton (right) was typically magnificent as he shredded Green Bay's defense for 192 yards—tying his third-best single-game performance—and the game-winning touchdown, a 27-yard run early in the fourth quarter. Along the way, Payton passed the 14,000-yard mark in his wondrous career as the Bears rolled on, 16-10.

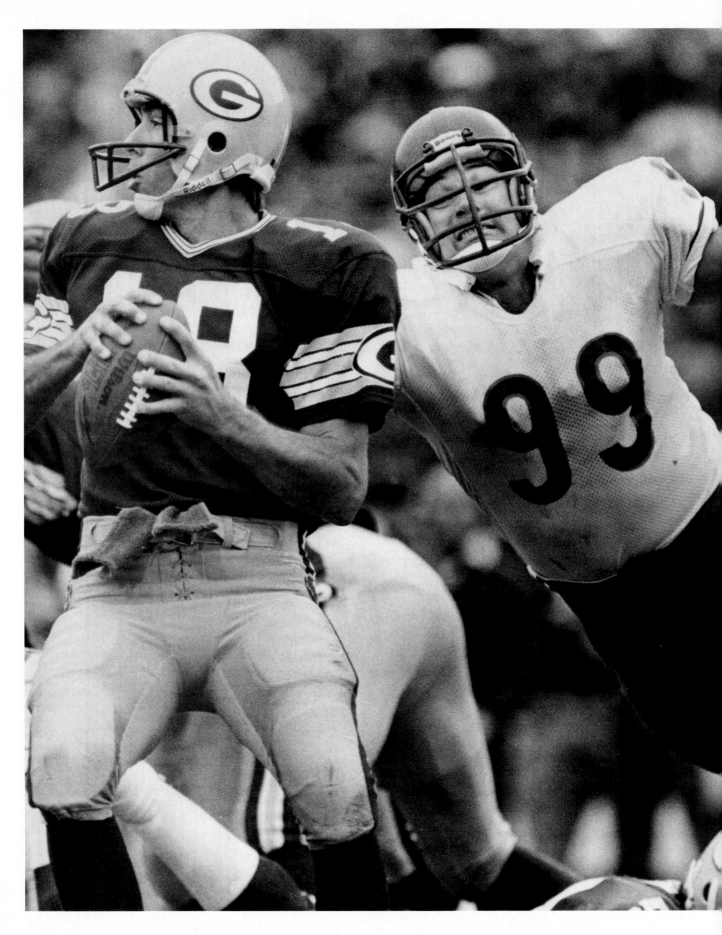

Bears defensive tackle Dan Hampton (left) smothered quarterback Jim Zorn, who was held to 11-of-26 passing, for one of his two sacks. The gap-toothed smile of William Perry (above) was prominent in the Bears' locker room after The Refrigerator's four-yard touchdown catch off a play-action pass provided Chicago with a 7-3 lead.

Seattle's spirited defense gave up 101 tough yards to Raiders running back Marcus Allen (right), but not much else in a 33-3 shellacking of Los Angeles. In all, the Seahawks had six sacks, four interceptions, and a blocked field goal that was returned 56 yards for a key touchdown.

Seahawks '85

Curt Warner couldn't do it alone. In their heads, the Seattle Seahawks knew that. In 1984, they had rallied to an inspiring 12-4 season without their star running back. Now that he was back from knee surgery, imagine where they'd go. Many picked them for the Super Bowl. Did they let down just a wee bit?

The first eight games were a harsh dose of reality. Seattle went 4-4 and gave up an average of 25 points a game. "It's a new season," coach Chuck Knox said, and darned if they didn't play with the old spirit in beating the Los Angeles Raiders 33-3. The old magic, too: turnovers and kicking teams.

In the 23-point second quarter, Terry Taylor blocked a field goal with his facemask and Byron Walker turned it into a 56-yard touchdown. Later, Taylor scored on a 75-yard interception return. Seattle had four interceptions, a fumble recovery, and six sacks.

There was still time. At 5-4, the Seahawks were one game off the division lead. But they couldn't get out of their rut, winning two and then losing two, for an 8-8 finish.

"Turnovers tell the story," Knox said. Seattle lost 23 interceptions and 18 fumbles, tying the most-ever committed by a Knox team. Its differential dropped from plus-24 to plus-3. Kicking teams declined, too.

The offense also was erratic. Seattle scored at least 24 in all its wins, but had 14 or less in six defeats. Even with Warner running for 1,094 yards, the running game tied for twenty-first. But there were enough bright days for Daryl Turner's league-leading 13 touchdown catches, for Steve Largent's league-leading 1,287 yards on 79 catches and record-tying seventh 1,000-yard season, and for hope.

Week 10

Bears 24, Lions 3

The last time Steve Fuller did anything but mop up, he was on the painful end of coach Mike Ditka's hook in the third game. The flip side of Jim McMahon's heroic coming-out party at Minnesota was Fuller's frustration at coming out after playing reasonably well. "Not exactly a confidence builder," he said.

Now he was starting again. McMahon was nursing tendinitis in his throwing shoulder. And Ditka was letting the air out of Fuller's balloon once more, with runs on the Bears' first 21 plays against the visiting Detroit Lions.

Nothing personal. Fuller understood. Running made sense against the Lions, whose cautious defense curtailed big plays but ranked last against the run. It made even more sense in a game in which the starting quarterback, tight end, and flanker did not play because of injuries. Throw in the 17 miles-per-hour wind, rain, and 39 degrees, and a big passing show was unthinkable.

Twelve of those first 21 plays came on the 63-yard drive that put the Bears ahead 7-0 late in the first quarter. They finished the game with 55 runs for 250 yards, 16 for 102 by Matt Suhey and 26 for 107 by Walter Payton. The 24-3 victory marked the third time in Payton's career that the Bears had two 100-yard runners.

All things considered, the game plan was more of a pat on Fuller's back than a slap in his face. It wasn't a hand-me-down from Mc-Mahon, for one thing. A year ago, Ditka hadn't tailored Fuller's game plans to his roll-out strengths, but this time Ditka had him circle the plays he liked best. Those were the ones Ditka called. "I do better if I move out of the pocket than if I sit back there and throw it all the time," Fuller said.

He scored the first and third touchdowns on bootleg runs, first with William Perry as a decoy and later after withholding a handoff to Payton that would have tested the teeth of Detroit's defense. His 13 passes included 7 completions for 112 yards and no interceptions.

"Coming into this game," Fuller said, "the Bears were 9-0 and Steve Fuller felt he hadn't done a whole lot to contribute to that success. Just a chance to be part of this makes me happy.

"I felt like there had been some doubt whether we could win without Jim. The idea we'd fall flat on our faces and not be able to do anything discouraged me a little bit. But the guys rallied around me and we did all right."

All along, the Bears' undefeated season had been on the line. Both lines, actually. The number-one defense against the run and soon-to-be-number-one rushing offense were perfectly suited for bad weather. When the Lions took the wind after winning the toss, the Bears let them have the ball for only 2:46 of the first quarter and only 18:58 of the game.

"Some of the holes were unbelievable," Fuller said. Most of them were between the tackles, where Suhey runs on nearly equal ground with Payton. Suhey had six of the 10 runs that gained 10 yards or more.

"Just goes to show you, Matt's always been a great running back," Payton said.

Suhey was the guy who said the best back-field of all time was Payton and whoever happened to be next to him. "Playing in a great city, getting paid fairly, playing with perhaps the greatest player ever in the game, what more could you ask for?" Suhey said.

It was the fifth time in a row the Bears gave up 10 points or less. The Lions scored only after Fuller lost an unwise lateral at the Bears' 33. The defense had four turnovers and four sacks, including two by Perry. The Lions had eight first downs and 106 yards.

"That many?" grumped Mike Singletary, who recovered two fumbles. "I was hoping we held them to about seventy-five." He meant it.

Bears safety Gary Fencik sent Detroit running back James Jones on his way to a crash landing in Chicago's 24-3 victory. The Lions were held to 106 yards in total offense, just 68 on the ground.

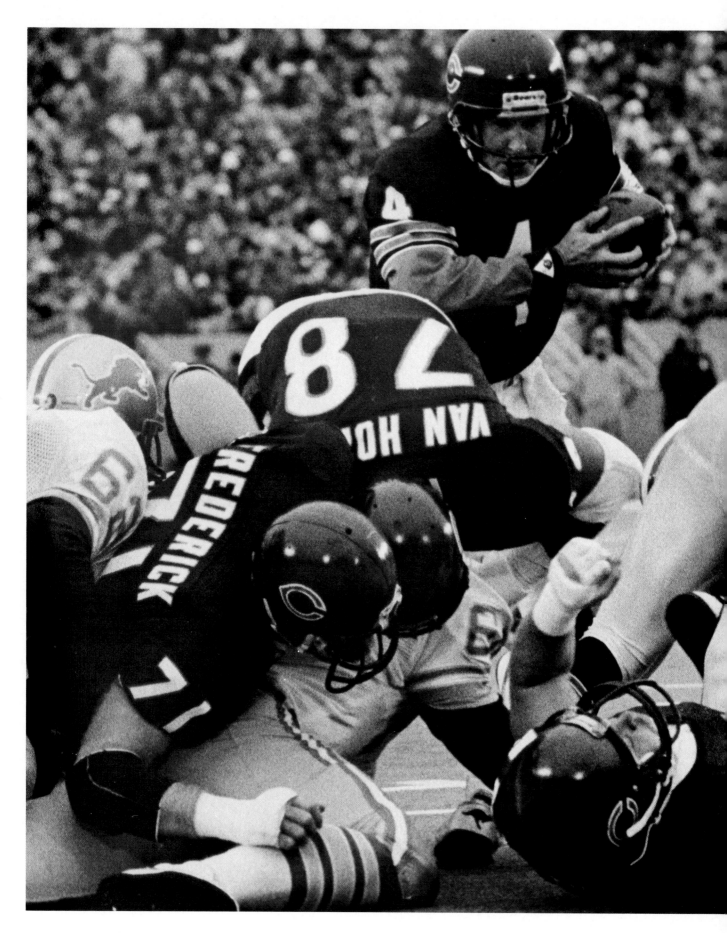

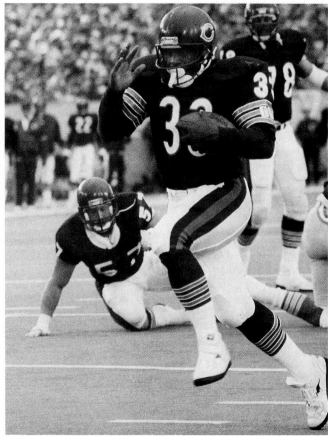

Backup quarterback Steve Fuller (left) did his best impression of Jim McMahon, who was sidelined with tendinitis in his shoulder. Fuller ran for two touchdowns, passed for 112 yards, and directed a potent offense. The Bears dominated in the trenches, rushing for 250 yards. Even rookie running back Calvin Thomas (above) got into the act, scampering seven yards for a second-quarter touchdown, his first as a pro.

Steelers '85

When the Steelers got rolling, they could make a team scurry for cover. Gary Anderson's team-record five field goals led them past Kansas City 36-28 for their first road victory. He led the AFC with 139 points. But Pittsburgh was only 5-5 after the game against the Chiefs. Its 6-5 mark the next week was its only visit above .500 in a 7-9 season, its first losing record since 1971.

Third-string quarterback Scott Campbell led a scoring outburst in week 15, when the Steelers overcame Buffalo's 21-0 lead and won 30-24. The smallest crowd in Three Rivers Stadium's 16 years angered Campbell by cheering the injuries to his predecessors, David Woodley and Mark Malone. Quarterbacks changed frequently. Even Woodley called Pittsburgh's offense conservative and predictable. Others criticized the Steelers' lack of mettle.

The Steelers lost 8 of 10 games that were decided in the fourth quarter. They didn't beat a team with a winning record.

Pittsburgh committed eight turnovers in seven victories, 28 in nine defeats. It lost seven of the eight times it gave up at least 24 points, hitting bottom in a 54-44 defeat at San Diego that made its record 6-8. The defense ranked sixth in yardage and second against the pass, but lacked big plays.

Wide receiver-punt returner Louis Lipps was electrifying again. He led the AFC with 15 touchdowns, including two on returns, and led all 50-catch receivers with a 19.2-yard average per catch. Veteran receiver John Stallworth added 75 receptions. Frank Pollard and Walter Abercrombie each ran for more than 850 yards. "This team is going to win again," Stallworth said. "Mark my words."

Pittsburgh won its first road game of the season, 36-28 in Kansas City, as former Baylor University running mates Walter Abercrombie (34, left) and Frank Pollard (30) combined for 120 yards rushing. Second-year wide receiver Louis Lipps put on a spectacular show for the Steelers, returning six punts for 128 yards, including a 71-yard touchdown (right) that gave Pittsburgh the lead for good. Lipps also caught three passes for 40 yards.

Week 11

Bears 44, Cowboys 0

For years, Bears general manager Jerry Vainisi had fantasized about seeing disgruntled Dallas Cowboys fans head for the Texas Stadium exits in the third quarter. Now it was happening, but linebacker Mike Singletary was shouting, "Stay here! I want witnesses!" Near the end of the Bears' shocking 44-0 victory, with the crowd's remnants cheering them on, Singletary turned to fellow Texan Steve McMichael and said, "I don't think I could have dreamed it any better."

The big showdown turned into a meltdown for the Cowboys' offense. The Bears didn't even give them a blindfold for their execution. They certainly didn't give them the run. Then they took away the pass, and, finally, their pride.

It was the Cowboys' worst defeat ever, their first shutout in 218 games and 15 years. Their deepest drive was to the Bears' 38-yard line, the first time they had the ball. "Our defense took the game away from them," coach Mike Ditka said. "It was awesome to see."

Ditka had often preached about rising to the level of an opponent. The example he usually used was Dallas, where he had played four years and coached for nine. Chicago players, who had lost six straight to the Cowboys since 1971, frankly grew tired of hearing about Dallas.

"If we'd gone 15-1 and lost to Dallas, it would have been, 'Man, you guys are real good, but you couldn't beat those Cowboys,'" Singletary said.

"Everybody wanted it, more so for Mike," Walter Payton said. But Ditka tried to make it just another game. The night before, he showed Rodney Dangerfield tapes at the pregame meeting. Even when the offense struggled in the first quarter, Ditka stayed cool.

Maybe he knew the defense had the game under control when it was 12 minutes old, even with the score 0-0. The Cowboys' first running play had gone 22 yards, but their next five netted minus-five, none crossing the line of scrimmage. The defense was shifting every time the offense shifted, fouling up blocking schemes. "I've never seen their offense so confused," safety Gary Fencik said.

The Cowboys had to pass, and the Bears knew they had to pass. None of Dallas's 16 offensive plays the rest of the first half were runs. They were sacked three times, completed 4 of 13 passes, and had three passes intercepted, two returned for touchdowns.

Defensive end Richard Dent scored first with 1:48 left in the first quarter. Maury Buford had punted the Cowboys back to their 2-yard line, and Danny White passed from the end zone. From his right, Dan Hampton tipped the ball high in the air. "Any time you hear the ball slapped, you're supposed to look for it," said Dent, who located the ball with the skill of a catcher under a pop foul and grabbed it at the 1 like a leaping rebounder. "My intention was getting it before anybody else noticed it."

Mike Richardson's touchdown came 11 minutes later on a 36-yard return. This was off Gary Hogeboom, who was hurried by Dent and Otis Wilson. Wilson had knocked White out of the game. He would do it again in the second half. "I put the wood on him," he said.

Hogeboom's next pass was a long one that Leslie Frazier intercepted. His 33-yard return through several Cowboys set up a 52-yard touchdown drive to make the halftime score 24-0.

This week's Refrigerator refrain featured William Perry picking Payton up at the Cowboys' 2-yard line to carry him into the end zone. It was illegal and earned a penalty. But it was fun. On his own, Payton's 132 yards gave him a record ninth 1,000-yard season and six straight 100-yard games, one short of the record.

The Bears' 11-0 record was the NFL's best since 1972. They were the first team to clinch a division so early in a 16-game season, but the only way they celebrated was to give each player a game ball.

Defensive end Richard Dent grabbed a deflected pass (right) thrown by Cowboys quarterback Danny White and stepped into the end zone for a one-yard interception return that gave Chicago a 7-0 lead late in the first quarter. The Bears never looked back, powering their way to a shocking 44-0 victory in Dallas.

The ubiquitous, blitzing Chicago defense, including Dan Hampton (99, above), Otis Wilson (55), and Wilber Marshall (58), harassed Cowboys quarterback Danny White all day and held the Cowboys to 119 yards passing, 171 overall. Walter Payton gained 132 yards, pushing his season total to 1,083, the ninth time he had gained at least 1,000 yards, an NFL record. On one run near the goal line, he even brought along a 308-pound bodyguard, William (The Refrigerator) Perry, who illegally attempted to carry Payton into the end zone (right) and earned a penalty.

"If you score sixty-two points, you'll have a tough time losing," Jets quarterback Ken O'Brien (below) said after throwing for 367 yards and five touchdowns in less than three quarters as New York gained a measure of revenge against Tampa Bay, 62-28. When running back Tony Paige scored with 1:14 to play (right), the Jets had passed the 60-point mark.

Jets '85

Wanting revenge and getting it are two different things. Getting it by a 62-28 score is a horse laugh.

The Jets remembered last year. They remembered how Tampa Bay had embarrassed them in the final game, letting them score so James Wilder would have another shot at the combined-yardage record. "I could not have dreamed up a better payback," defensive tackle Barry Bennett said after the rout at the Meadowlands. The Jets scored on five consecutive possessions after trailing 14-0.

They set team records for points, first downs (35), and yards (581). Ken O'Brien gained 367 on a 23-for-30 passing day. His five touchdowns included three to Mickey Shuler, who wound up second among NFL tight ends with 76 catches. The Jets beat Tampa Bay largely without running back Freeman McNeil, who finished fifth in the NFL in rushing with 1,331 yards. O'Brien went on to lead NFL passers with a 96.2 rating and a touchdown-interception ratio of 25-8.

In one year, the offense leaped from sixteenth to fourth in yardage and from fifteenth to seventh in scoring. But the defense had even more to do with the surge from two 7-9 seasons, including seven losses in the last eight 1984 games, to 11-5 and a wild card. The defensive rankings zoomed from twentieth to third in scoring and twenty-first to eighth in yardage—third against the run.

The new defensive wizard was Bud Carson, who had coached Super Bowl defenses for the Steelers and Rams. He switched to a 3-4, made Joe Klecko a nose tackle at a 45-degree angle to the line, and moved star pass rusher Mark Gastineau around. The Jets held seven teams to 14 points or fewer.

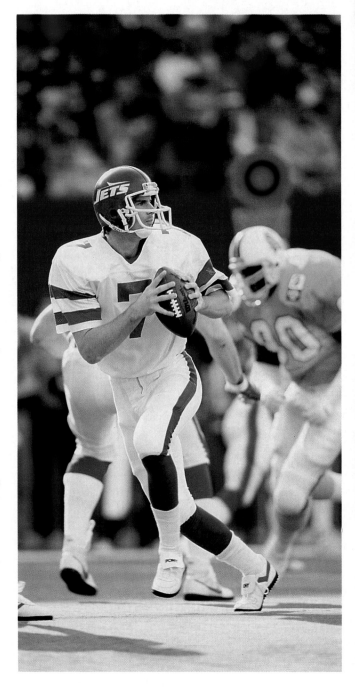

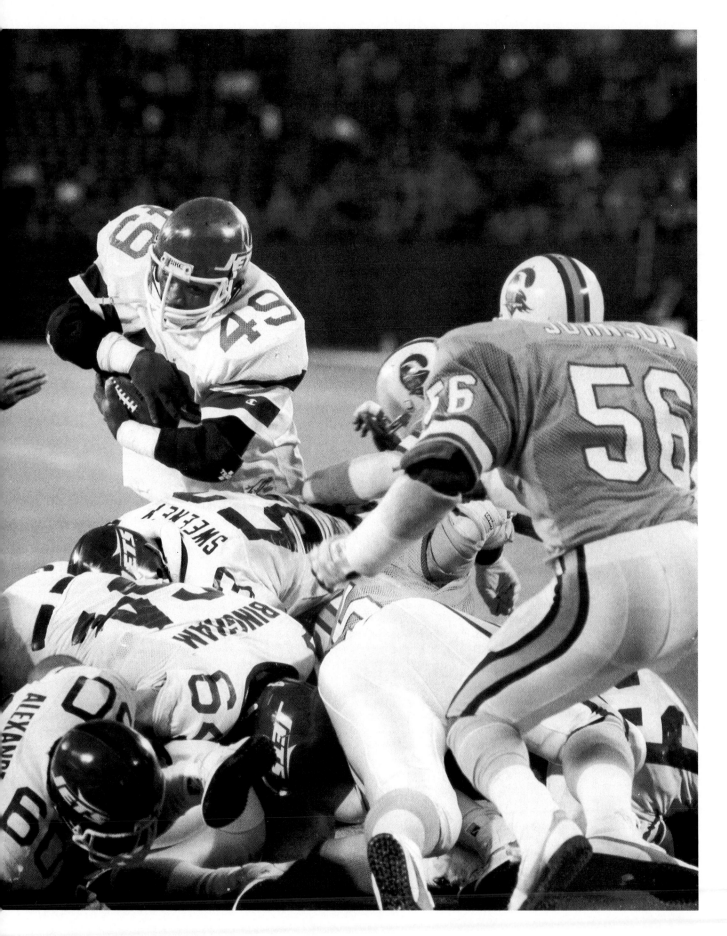

Week 12

Bears 36, Falcons 0

The question was whether the Bears' defense could play a perfect game. The Rams had held Seattle to minus-seven yards in 1979, but they had given up one first down. "Then it wasn't perfect," coach Mike Ditka concluded.

Nor was the 36-0 victory over Atlanta at Soldier Field, which made the Bears the third 12-0 team in NFL history. It was close, though. The Falcons' passing yardage was minus-22. Quarterback David Archer was lifted in the third quarter for his own protection after completing 1 of 14 passes for one yard and throwing two interceptions. Archer and Bob Holly were sacked five times, including three by defensive tackle Henry Waechter, who scored the Bears' third safety in six games. Chicago's defense had scored 27 points in those six games, the same number it had allowed. In three games in which backup quarterback Steve Fuller filled in for the injured Jim McMahon, the Bears had outscored their opponents 104-3.

It was time to start talking about the Bears as a team for the ages in pro football. "Our defense just ripped them apart," Ditka said. "They must have felt like it was Sherman's army marching through them."

The Falcons had 10 first downs and 119 yards. But middle linebacker Mike Singletary again was inconsolable in victory. He rated the defense a 7 on a scale of 10. It enraged him that Gerald Riggs's 30 carries produced 110 yards. "Some of the guys were teasing me about that," Singletary said. "They said, 'We still got 'em on the scoreboard.' But still!"

Before the San Francisco game, 49ers coach Bill Walsh said coordinator Buddy Ryan's defense looked vulnerable because its all-out pass rush and tight coverage were so extreme. But he said Ryan simply puts players where the offense wants to go.

That's why the 46—the centerpiece of the Bears' defensive smorgasbord—was getting copied faster than Madonna's wardrobe. It creates one-on-one matchups and unusual blocking needs by putting players over everyone but the strongside tackle, ordinarily a drive-blocking specialist who's not used to being left without an opponent to block.

But where other teams copied the alignments and blitzes, they didn't have the Bears' 14 coverage schemes off the 46. They didn't have players and coaches who had eight years' experience with the 46. Ryan had his players believing not only in the 46, but in his knack for pulling something else out of his bag of tricks if the opponent's offense was moving. He also had linebackers with the unusual speed to meet the 46's demands in pass coverage, sometimes against wide receivers.

On offense, the Bears never gave up the ball inside their 45. They scored four straight times for a 20-0 halftime lead. When two drives stalled, Kevin Butler's field goals made him 15 for 16 in the last nine games. Chicago's second-stringers won a 9-0 fourth quarter after outscoring Dallas 14-0 the week before.

Walter Payton made it 13-0 with a 40-yard touchdown, his longest run of the season, on a remarkable tightrope dash down the sideline. With 102 yards in three quarters, Payton tied Earl Campbell's and O.J. Simpson's record of seven straight 100-yard games, a record Ditka promised to break because Payton's name belonged "above those other backs."

Two Bears plays later, Willie Gault's 50-yard catch set up William Perry's one-yard touchdown leap. He said he decided to sprout wings after Dallas had stopped him from the 2 by hitting him low.

It was all starting to look so easy. "You look at the scoreboard and pinch yourself," Gary Fencik said.

"I know this team still hasn't put everything together yet," Payton said. "It's scary."

In a battle of standout running backs at Soldier Field, the Atlanta Falcons' young star, Gerald Riggs (right), picked up 110 yards on 30 carries to increase his league-leading rushing total to 1,248 yards. The Bears' Walter Payton carried 20 times for 102 yards to tie an NFL record with his seventh-consecutive 100-yard game.

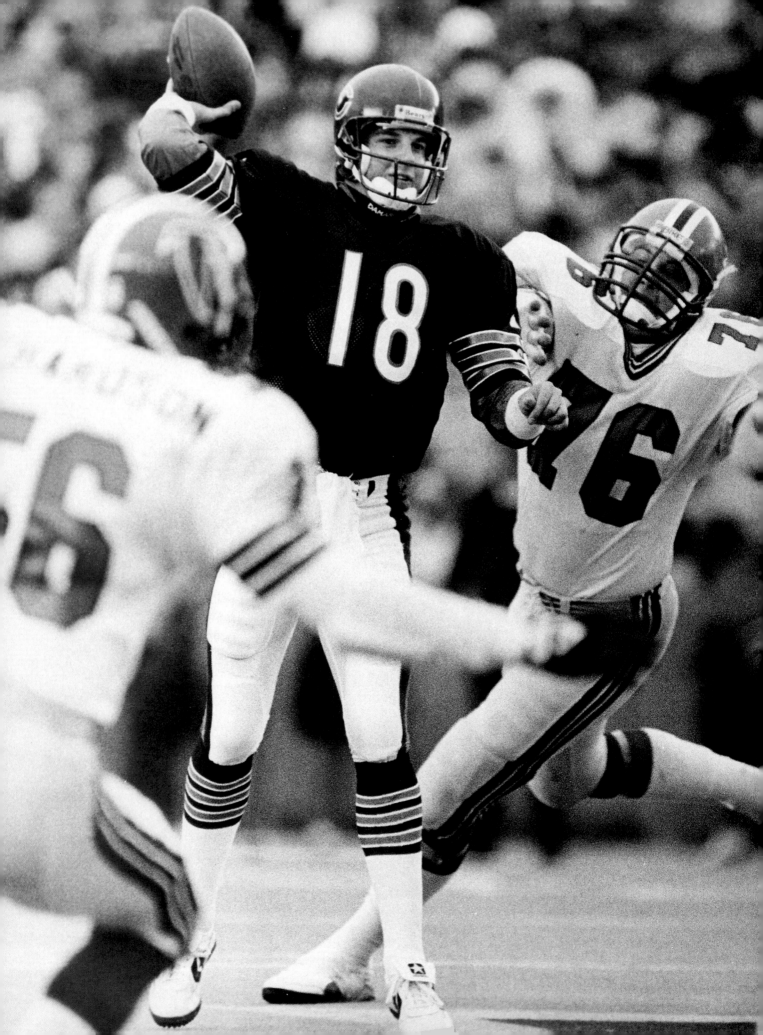

Even free-agent rookie quarterback Mike Tomczak (left) got into the act as the Bears breezed to their twelfth consecutive victory and second-successive shutout, 36-0. Tomczak completed 3 of 5 passes for 45 yards. When William Perry (below) took a one-yard touchdown plunge, it capped a 20-point second quarter and gave Chicago a 20-0 halftime lead over Atlanta.

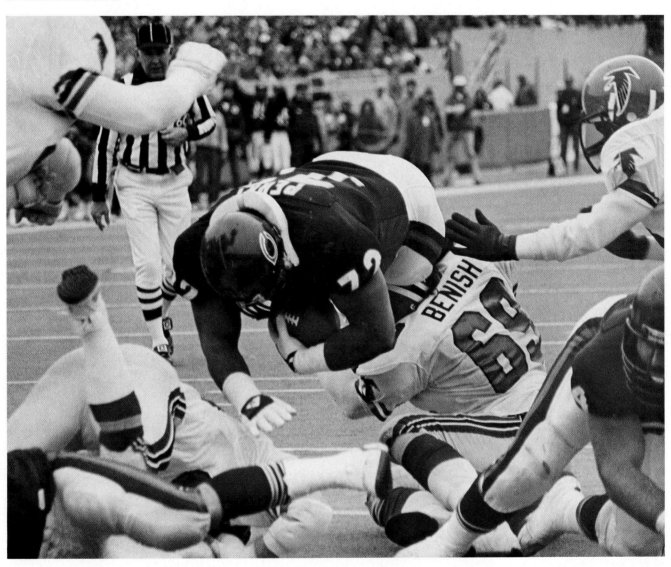

Raiders '85

Another overtime game against Denver. Last year, the Los Angeles Raiders had lost one when they fumbled in field-goal range. This time, they kicked on third down. Chris Bahr's 32-yarder made up for his miss at the end of regulation and the Raiders won 31-28. They tied the Broncos for first place in the AFC West at 8-4, and broke the tie two weeks later by beating Denver 17-14 in another overtime, then clinched the division the following week.

The Raiders finished 12-4 with six consecutive victories and 11 of 13. They won in a way they'd never won before—ball control and defense.

Their style started changing when they were 1-2, when quarterback Jim Plunkett dislocated his shoulder and Marc Wilson replaced him. Coach Tom Flores's staff called the plays for the first time. They mostly called them for Marcus Allen. Soon, he was carrying 27 times a game.

Allen ran 380 times for 1,759 yards and the Raiders' first NFL rushing championship. He scored 14 touchdowns. He added 67 catches, and his 2,314 combined yards set an NFL record. He tied Walter Payton's weeks-old record with nine consecutive 100-yard games.

Wilson was near the bottom of NFL passers all season, but he made game-winning plays and his ball-control passing made Todd Christensen the leading receiver among tight ends with 82 catches.

The Raiders won their last three games without scoring more than 17 points. They gave up 125 points in 12 victories, ranked second in sacks with 65, and fourth in yardage allowed. "We're a defensive team," linebacker Matt Millen said. "We're going to have to play great defensive football if we're going to have a chance to win."

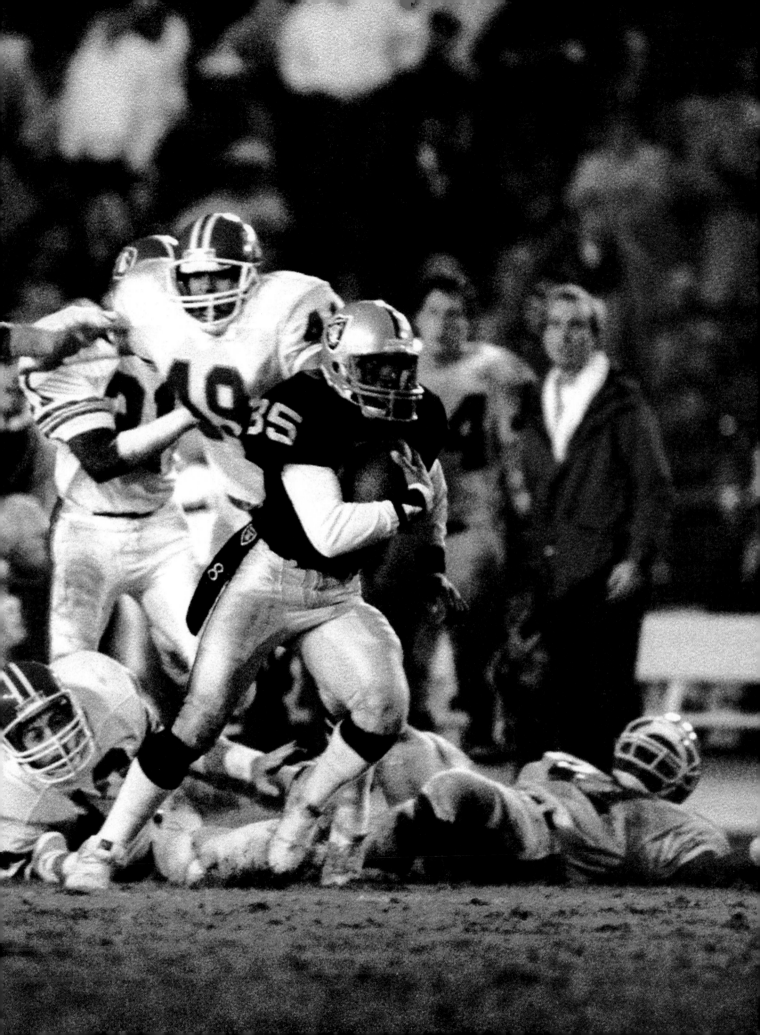

Week 13

Dolphins 38, Bears 24

Miami was bracing for the Bears as though they were a hurricane. Compared to the hype for their Monday night game, the promotion for new Coca-Cola was a classified ad. Radio stations played mostly songs about defrosting The Refrigerator. A newspaper carried hopeless readers' advice for the Dolphins, such as hijacking the Bears' bus. A TV station asked a Miami zookeeper if bears ate dolphins or vice versa, the sort of inanity usually reserved for Super Bowl weeks. This from a city whose team had been in five real Super Bowls.

The Bears had arrived. They finally had the national respect they had sought by grabbing opponents by the throat and fans by the heart. Oh, they were sure the ABC announcers hated them, but they had to have a *few* dragons to slay. There was growing consensus the NFL needn't bother with the formality of a Super Bowl to crown the Bears champions.

All that changed after Miami whipped them 38-24. The Dolphins led 17-7 just seven seconds into the second quarter. They scored every time they had the ball in the first half. They jumped ahead 31-10, scoring one more point than the Bears had allowed in seven games. Quarterback Dan Marino finished 14 for 27 for 270 yards and three touchdowns.

The fairy tale season was over. Miami preserved its record for the best NFL season. The 1972 Dolphins' 14-0 regular season and 17-0 overall would stand alone.

Had the pressure gotten to them? Hardly. This team was looser than the Pentagon's budget. "I think the pressure is on the people playing us," coach Mike Ditka had said that week.

Were they too cocky then? Possibly. The players were spending more time on TV commercials than on game film. The day before the Atlanta game, 10 of them had cut a record called "The Super Bowl Shuffle." Twenty-four would make the video the day after the Miami game.

"Any time you start patting yourself on the back, you've only got one hand to play with," said Dan Hampton, the only Bear who turned down a lead "Shuffle" role. "We'll talk about how good we are when it's all over. Any time you worry about looking in the rear-view mirror more than looking in the windshield, that's when you're going to run off the road."

Miami didn't find some secret way to beat the Bears, Ditka and defensive coordinator Buddy Ryan insisted. The Bears beat themselves. They allowed Marino to roll out all the way to the sideline on three big third-and-long plays. Players had been assigned the responsibility to contain him each time, but didn't.

On Miami's first touchdown drive, Marino passed for 30 yards on third-and-18. On its second, he passed for 22 on third-and-19 and 17 on second-and-18. On its third, he passed for 52 on third-and-13 and 26 on third-and-7. The fourth touchdown by Miami went six yards after William Judson's blocked punt and prompted a shouting match between two frustrated coaches, Ditka and Ryan.

Ditka admitted he could have been smarter, too, by staying out of a shootout with Marino. Walter Payton's first carry came 9½ minutes into the game. The blocked punt followed three failed pass plays with 1:28 left in the first half, when Payton ran only 10 times.

Payton broke the NFL record in the final minute with his eighth consecutive 100-yard game. Miami had been unable to run out the clock after Payton fumbled with 98 yards. He wound up with 121 yards for the night.

Jim McMahon played quarterback after Steve Fuller sprained his ankle with 12:47 to play. But there were no miracles this time. His only good drive ended with Miami's third interception. In their first 12 games, the Bears threw nine. "The interesting thing," Ditka said, "will be to see how we bounce back from this."

The defense sparkled in Miami's triumph, especially cornerback William Judson. He blocked Maury Buford's punt (left), which led to a Dolphins touchdown, intercepted a fourth-quarter pass (above), and had four solo tackles and two passes defensed. It was a victory for protectionism; the only perfect season in NFL history, the 17-0 compiled by Miami in 1972, was safe.

Broncos '85

John Elway was coming along just fine. He wasn't as spectacular as 1983 draft classmate Dan Marino, maybe, but Denver's sixth-ranked passing game kept it in the playoff race all season. Elway carried a team that didn't have a running back in the NFL's top 26 and had less bite on defense than the previous year, when the Broncos were 13-3. Their takeaways slipped from 55 to 36, and they allowed 88 more points than 1984's AFC-low 241.

The 31-23 victory at Pittsburgh was "a big step in John's development," coach Dan Reeves said. Elway had provided Pittsburgh a 23-17 lead on a 35-yard interception return with 5:02 to play. It had to remind Elway of the 1984 playoffs, when his late interception decided a loss to Pittsburgh. But this time, in front of a hostile crowd, "He just forgot about the interception and moved forward," Reeves said. Elway set up Denver's touchdown with a 27-yard pass.

Karl Mecklenburg played seven defensive line and linebacker positions in the game, as he did all season, and had four of his season's team-record 13 sacks. The defense was still a force.

Elway's next big step was against Kansas City in week 15. He threw five interceptions and heard hometown boos before completing eight straight passes on the last two drives in a 14-13 comeback victory. "I grew from that," Elway said the next week, when he brought Denver from 0-17 to a 27-24 victory at Seattle.

With an 11-5 record, the Broncos could only wait for Sunday's results. To make the playoffs, they needed either the Jets or the Patriots to lose. Both won. The Broncos became the first 11-5 team ever to miss the playoffs.

Denver remained in a first-place tie with the Raiders, while the Steelers fell a game behind in the AFC Central as quarterback John Elway (below) led the Broncos to a 31-23 victory in Pittsburgh. ''This was Elway's finest hour,'' Denver coach Dan Reeves said after Elway passed for 238 yards and superbly directed a late rally. Linebacker Mike Merriweather (right, tackling Sammy Winder) had given the Steelers a 23-17 lead by returning an interception 35 yards for a touchdown with 5:02 to play.

Week 14

Bears 17, Colts 10

What now? The Bears had clinched the home field through the playoffs a week earlier, when the Rams lost the day before the Miami game. They couldn't go undefeated anymore. They had run out of points to prove but still had three meaningless games to play.

Gary Fencik was encouraged before the game against Indianapolis. The players were unusually quiet during the Soldier Field warmups. "I thought it meant we were saving it for the game," he said. "Then we got out there and stayed quiet the whole first half. It was time to start barking a little bit."

They were flat for their 17-10 victory. Football players rarely admit to being flat, even if a draftsman mistakes them for his table. They say the other team made them look that bad. The Bears came clean. They said they were flat.

"Wasn't it obvious?" tackle Keith Van Horne asked.

"That's the first time on the sidelines that I thought everybody was playing with pillows in front of them," coach Mike Ditka said. "I couldn't hear anybody hitting out there. We looked like we were pushing instead of really coming out on people."

The thing that almost escaped attention was that they won this horrible game. That's how far the Bears had come. They had recent 5-9 teams that didn't feel as bad about losing as this 13-1 bunch felt about winning.

The fans still loved them. They were offering William Perry $5,000 to sign autographs in shopping centers. They were forming a troupe of overweight cheerleaders called the Refrigerettes. The Art Institute even ordered 50-pound Bears helmets to put on its Colossal Lions, the statues on so many Chicago post cards. By the end of the weekend, both helmets were stolen.

The halftime boos were more from fear than loathing. Chicago fans had allowed DePaul, the White Sox, and the Cubs to lift their spirits, only to drop them with a splat. *Et tu*, Bears?

The Colts game was the first time all season that the Bears' defense made no turnovers. Its only sack was late in the game. The longest play on offense was 30 yards. They didn't have any big plays. That's the difference between an eye-popping 44-0 victory and an eye-closing 17-10.

The Bears ultimately took this one by taking the ball away. The score was 3-3 midway through the third quarter. Walter Payton had run for 18 yards. The rest of the way, the Bears controlled the ball for 18:40 and let the Colts have it for 3:54. Their two 5½-minute touchdown drives made it 17-3. They went from finesse plays to straight-ahead power and Payton wound up with 111 yards, 61 in the fourth quarter. "We did what we had to do to win," Payton said.

Both touchdown drives were set up by Maury Buford's punts to the Colts' 4-yard line. Payton ran for the tiebreaker late in the third quarter, 16 yards from Shotgun formation on third-and-six. "They thought we were going to pass and just vacated," he said. "Perry could have gone through that hole."

Questions remained. The loss at Miami had put the Bears' blemishes under harsher light. Minor blemishes, sure, but this was Mike Pagel scrambling outside containment, not Dan Marino. It was Wayne Capers catching a late 61-yard touchdown pass, not Mark Duper. "We're going to see those rollouts until we stop them," Fencik said.

And whatever became of that new passing attack? Jim McMahon was back at quarterback, his first start in five weeks. He said his shoulder felt fine, but Payton had to pull the game out. The Bears had gained 7.7 yards per pass play in the first six games, but only 5.5 in the last eight.

"Maybe it's hard to play with intensity, knowing we're in the playoffs," Fencik said. "But if we play like this, we won't be around long in January."

Indianapolis rookie linebacker Duane Bickett put the slug on quarterback Jim McMahon (right). The Bears were tied 3-3 at halftime and struggled all day before holding on for a 17-10 victory, their first over the Colts in a regular-season game since 1966.

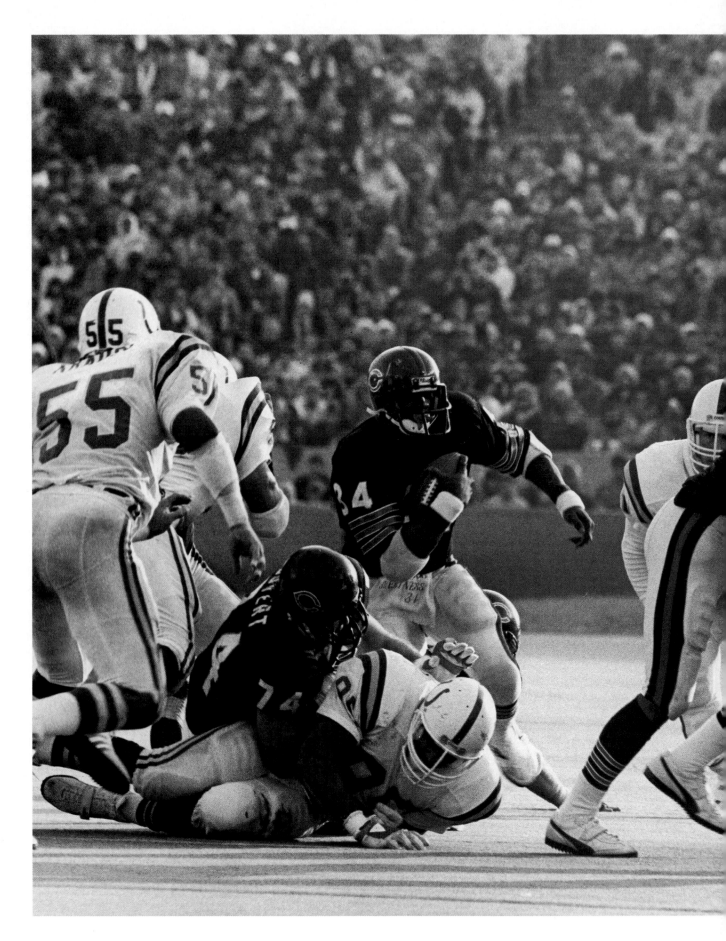

A model of consistency, Walter Payton (left) rushed for 111 yards, including 61 in the fourth quarter. Battling the flu, Payton nevertheless started his one-hundred fiftieth game in a row, and also extended his NFL record of consecutive 100-yard games to nine. Maury Buford (above) gave the Bears good field position all during the game, averaging 44 yards on his four punts.

Bengals '85

From any perspective, the Bengals were scary. They made Tom Landry a believer when they thumped a good Dallas team 50-24. They started with a quick safety, made it 9-0 with a no-huddle touchdown drive, then went ahead 22-0 after 8:47. With 12 minutes left, it was 50-10. Their 570 yards were the most-ever against Dallas.

But the Bengals weren't always a pretty sight from the Cincinnati sideline. The next week, they jumped ahead 24-7 in the first half at Washington, only to lose 27-24. Against the Giants earlier, their 21-0 lead shrank to 21-20 before they won 35-30. They lost by scores of 44-41, 41-27, and 44-27 to teams that didn't have winning seasons.

The Bengals ranked third in the NFL in scoring, but third from the bottom in points allowed. That's why they finished 7-9.

Another reason was their slow-start habit. They could explain their 1-6 starts of the previous two years by pointing to player suspensions and a new coach. But this time, they stumbled out of the blocks at 2-5 despite a defense that returned intact. After giving up more than 27 points just twice in 1984, the Bengals did it six times in their first seven games of 1985. After that, they went to a Bear-like 46 defense, using younger and faster linebackers.

If anything, it was Cincinnati's offense that figured to start slowly. Quarterback Boomer Esiason was in his second year, wide receiver Eddie Brown was a rookie, and running back James Brooks had struggled in 1984. But the Bengals scored at least 20 points in all but the two six-point games that dropped them from 5-5 to 5-7. Esiason's 93.2 rating ranked second among NFL passers.

Week 15

Bears 19, Jets 6

Time for a pre-playoff tune-up. The New York weather was right, 35 degrees and a 19-miles-per-hour wind gusting to 28. So was the team. The Jets were 10-4, fighting for the AFC East lead, and had "the best defense we've faced all year," center Jay Hilgenberg said.

But the Bears' defense was better. It was harder to run through than a crowded church pew, and blustery games have to be won on the ground. The Bears' defense dominated the 19-6 victory, safety Dave Duerson said, so thoroughly that "from the third quarter on, it was just a matter of killing the clock."

"After a few plays, you know what you're going to be able to do or not," said defensive end Richard Dent, who drove left tackle Reggie McElroy out of the game. "I had a feeling right away we could shut them down."

Control is the key to bad-weather games. Ball control, of which the Bears had 39:36 minutes, and control of the lines, where the Bears' defense won and their offense tied. Having such control is especially important with the wind in your face, as it was for the Bears in the first and third quarters.

The offense took care of the first quarter, keeping the ball for 11:10 with two drives that made the score 10-3 early in the second quarter. When the offense struggled in the third quarter, the defense took over. Dent ended two straight New York possessions by punching the ball from quarterback Ken O'Brien on sacks. With league leads in rushing offense, rushing defense, and takeaways, the Bears checked out for bad weather like Alaskan huskies.

"I'd be miserable playing at home in January," Dan Hampton had said. "But I'd much rather be miserable here than go out and get beat in L.A. Then I'd really be miserable."

It would be much worse in the playoffs. "Chicago in January, Vaseline freezes," Dent said.

Playoff games are *supposed* to be cold, mid-dle linebacker Mike Singletary said. He remembered watching snow-belt games as a kid, before domes and AstroTurf ruined them. "It was always the middle linebacker standing right in the middle and snow and everything blowing everywhere. Oh, that's great. Mud and blood flying everywhere. That's it! I love it."

The defense showed it could beat a playoff team without much help from the offense. "People were beginning to wonder," cornerback Leslie Frazier said. After two lackluster games, coordinator Buddy Ryan's reservations were so strong that he gave the defenders three written tests on the game plan for the Jets.

It was the fifth time the Bears held an offense without a touchdown, something that hadn't happened to the Jets since their opener. They were the eleventh Chicago opponent to score 10 points or less. It was a good thing, too, because nine of Walter Payton's 28 carries lost yardage. "I felt like a punching bag," Payton said after his record streak of nine 100-yard games ended with 53 yards.

Kicking was another edge the Bears had for bad weather. Two of Kevin Butler's four field goals were into the wind, including a 31-yarder after the Jets pulled within 10-6. Ditka let him kick a 21-yarder with 17 seconds left to set a Bears record with 12 in a row. At 28 for 33, he was three past the Bears' record for field goals in a season. He led the league with 131 points, one behind Gale Sayers's record for NFL rookies. And his 21-for-22 success since the third game was minimizing the problem of drives dying inside the 20-yard line, which happened five of six times at New York.

All season, Butler made a point of congratulating the offensive linemen after every field goal. "They're the guys who do all the work," he said. As winter and the playoffs approached, the Bears had the linemen who could harvest victories from frozen fields.

The Jets hadn't lost at home this season . . . until the Bears hit town. Then New York's Ken O'Brien, the NFL's top-rated quarterback, ran into Dan Hampton (right) and the NFL's top-rated defense on a windy day at the Meadowlands. What followed wasn't a pretty sight for Jets fans. O'Brien was sacked four times, fumbled twice, and was held to 122 yards on 12-of-26 passing. Pages 134-135: All season long, the Bears' offensive line had performed at a high level of efficiency and intensity. With tackle Keith Van Horne (78) leading the way, fullback Matt Suhey charged through a gaping hole in the Jets' defense. Suhey picked up 23 yards on seven carries.

It was a rainy Monday night in the Orange Bowl for the American Football Conference East showdown between Miami and New England. Still, the Dolphins' Dan Marino (below) connected on 17 of 33 passes for 192 yards, including several on the drive that led to Fuad Reveiz's game-winning, 47-yard field goal with 4:27 left. Tony Eason tried to bring the Patriots back, but safety Glenn Blackwood (right) intercepted his second pass of the night with 56 seconds left to clinch the victory.

Dolphins '85

It didn't look as easy for the Dolphins this time around. Even when they knocked New England out of the AFC East race, all but clinching it with one game left, they blew a 27-13 lead in the fourth quarter. Rookie Fuad Reveiz's 47-yard field goal won it 30-27.

"We always find ways to keep 'em interesting," Miami coach Don Shula said after Glenn Blackwood's second interception stopped the Patriots' last-ditch drive. It was the Dolphins' eighteenth-consecutive home victory against New England. They would finish their fifth straight season atop the AFC East with a 12-4 record and a seven-game winning streak.

They had come a long way since Houston shocked them 26-23 in the opener. Quarterback Dan Marino had held out of training camp for 37 days, yet went on to lead the league with 4,137 passing yards and 30 touchdowns. But Miami's passing yardage slipped to second in the NFL.

Much of the problem stemmed from Mark Duper's hairline leg fracture early in the second game. When he returned, the Dolphins were 5-4 and in third place. It might have been worse without rookie Ron Davenport's goal-line offense for 13 touchdowns, and Reveiz's 22 for 27 on field goals.

Duper came back against the first-place Jets in week 10. Like New England, New York already had beaten Miami. The Jets were leading 17-14 when Miami got possession of the ball with 1:08 to play.

Duper was hurting. But from the 50, he raced past cornerback Bobby Jackson, jumped for a fingertip catch, and scored the winning touchdown. Combined with his earlier 60-yard touchdown, his 217 yards on eight catches set a team record.

Week 16

Bears 37, Lions 17

The celebration was canceled on account of the blizzard that stormed from coach Mike Ditka. He was furious, 15-1 team or not. "Terrified," he said. The whole point of going 15-1 was to hit the playoffs at full speed, and the Bears had just staggered through their last game at Detroit. The specter of 15-2 was a recurring nightmare.

When he was reminded the Bears had beaten Detroit 37-17 in the Silverdome, he said, "So what? You saw the game."

Ditka saw his team commit four turnovers and score only two touchdowns on eight trips past the Lions' 30-yard line. He saw it blow the NFL pass defense lead by giving up 253 yards, despite six sacks. He saw it lead only 6-3 at halftime and 16-10 after three quarters.

The players were stunned at his outburst. They were ready for the playoffs, they said. My goodness, they were the second team ever to win 15 regular-season games, the first since 1973 to go undefeated within the NFC Central Division, the toast of Chicago. "You'd think we went 1-15 instead of 15-1," Gary Fencik said.

"There's nothing to be sad about," linebacker Otis Wilson said. "We haven't been dominating people like we did before, but it's a long season. We're human beings. We're not robots. I'm going to buy my kids robots for Christmas. They're going to be perfect. Until the batteries run out."

The point to Ditka's tirade was that the Bears should not be satisfied with their near-perfect record. "Maybe other coaches would be satisfied," he said. "Maybe I'm a perfectionist."

That's what got the Bears this far. They played the season above ordinary standards— scoring 30 points and grousing that it could have been 60, pitching a shutout and apologizing for all the yards they gave up.

Other teams might be satisfied to have good players at every position, great ones at many. The Bears wanted *two* good players everywhere. Lots of places, they had them. When Mike Single-

tary sprained a knee early in the second half, Ron Rivera replaced him at middle linebacker. Later, Rivera scored a touchdown. He was the twenty-first Bear to score, the ninth who was not a starter. Dennis Gentry's 94-yard return of the second-half kickoff kept the Bears ahead through three quarters, and he wasn't even their main return man.

Other teams might be satisfied scoring 28.5 points a game, second in the league. But the Bears were embarrassed by all their fizzled drives close to the goal line. "The story of our season," quarterback Jim McMahon said. "We've got to get better. Six points at halftime is ridiculous. We were lucky to win."

Other teams might be satisfied climbing from twenty-third to third against the pass in the last eight games. "We'll just have to work harder next year," Dan Hampton said after the Bears missed a triple league lead in total, rushing, and passing defense.

Other teams might be satisfied if their players follow assignments. The Bears expect more. Linebacker Wilber Marshall was in pass coverage on the game's third play. But his man stayed back to block, so he barged in and clobbered quarterback Joe Ferguson, who had to leave the game.

McMahon was supposed to pass on third-and-goal from the 14, early in the fourth quarter. But the receiver was covered and he noticed an opening, so he ran for the touchdown.

Two plays later, defensive end Richard Dent made a good play containing James Jones for no gain on a sideline pass. He also punched the ball away and blocked Jones while Rivera scored. Two big plays in less than a minute put the Bears ahead 30-10 with 13:16 to play.

A few days later, Matt Suhey said, "A lot of guys are scared to death of losing in the playoffs." Ditka had the players right where he wanted them. "That's how they should feel," he said.

Tuning up for their Super Bowl run, the Bears concluded a 15-1 regular season by hammering Detroit 37-17 at the Silverdome. Jim McMahon's 14-yard touchdown run (right) triggered a 21-point outburst in the fourth quarter. Unimpressed, Bears coach Mike Ditka said: "I'm extremely concerned about this team. The way we're playing, we'll never get to the Super Bowl."

The Patriots' plight was simple: Beat Cincinnati in the sub-freezing temperatures of Foxboro, Massachusetts, and make the playoffs as a wild-card team. Mission accomplished. Relying on their powerful ground attack, which featured guard John Hannah (73) and running back Tony Collins (33), among others, New England pounded the Bengals for 281 yards en route to a 34-23 victory.

Patriots '85

The team looked like so many other New England disappointments, especially when it started 2-3. The only obvious change was Raymond Berry, the Hall of Fame receiver, in his first full season as head coach. "He's made a big difference," cornerback Raymond Clayborn said after the Patriots' 11-5 wild-card season, their best in seven years.

"He told us we were good enough to win if we did what he asked," Pro Bowl tackle Brian Holloway said. "When players hear his words and know he has walked in the shoes he is asking and demanding of you, it has a lot of meaning."

The Patriots still could have missed the playoffs by losing their last game against Cincinnati. Their 20-6 halftime lead dwindled to 27-23 late in the fourth quarter. But they put it away 34-23, when a fourth-and-inches call to Robert Weathers went for a 42-yard score.

Eleven weeks earlier, Cleveland had beaten the Patriots on a fourth-and-inches tackle at the goal line. Linebacker Andre Tippett, who had another sensational season, threw helmets around the locker room and yelled at teammates to look in the mirror for someone to blame. The Patriots won their next six games. The defense wound up ranked sixth in scoring and seventh in yardage. Tippett's 16½ sacks led the AFC.

But the winning streak belonged mostly to quarterback Steve Grogan. His 18-game layoff ended when Tony Eason suffered a separated shoulder in week 6. The Patriots didn't lose again until Grogan suffered a hairline fracture of his left leg in week 12.

Grogan leaned on Craig James, who ran for 1,227 yards with a career-high 142 in the last game.

Wide receiver Stephone Paige (right), signed by the Chiefs as an undrafted free agent in 1983, set an all-time NFL record in the season finale against San Diego. Paige, a 6-1, 180-pounder, gained 309 yards receiving, on eight catches, breaking the mark of 303 yards by Jim Benton of the Cleveland Rams in 1945. Included among his receptions were touchdown catches of 56 and 84 yards.

Chiefs '85

Maybe Stephone Paige's spectacular finish will make next year easier to wait for in Kansas City, coming as it did in the final game.

Just before halftime, Paige, signed two years earlier as an undrafted free agent, had to be helped off the field with bruised ribs. The wide receiver already had six pass receptions for 258 yards, a team record by 45 yards. The game meant nothing. The Chiefs were comfortably ahead, although San Diego would squeeze Kansas City's early 35-3 lead to 38-34 at the end.

Paige returned midway through the third quarter. He gained another 39 yards. He didn't think he could continue. Then someone told him he was six yards from the NFL record of 303. ''My ribs really hurt,'' he said later. ''But when I found out how close I was, my ribs stopped hurting. I just sucked it up and went for it.'' Paige's eighth catch gained 12 yards. He had 309. Jim Benton, an old Cleveland Ram, had held the record since 1945.

It was bittersweet consolation for a team that started 3-1, beating the Raiders and Seahawks convincingly. The Chiefs talked about making the playoffs for the first time in 14 years. Then the balloon popped. They lost their next seven.

Third-year quarterback Todd Blackledge offered a glimmer of hope. The Chiefs went 3-2 when he started the last five games in place of injured Bill Kenney. Nick Lowery's 24 for 27 on field goals was an .889 percentage, third best in NFL history. Cornerback Albert Lewis's eight interceptions tied for the AFC lead. Paige scored on 10 of his 43 catches, with a dazzling 21.9-yard average. Veteran running back Mike Pruitt was the Chiefs' first 100-yard rusher in 55 games in week 14.

The 1985 Playoffs

SURPRISE PARTIES & BEARS' BLANKS

AFC Wild Card

Patriots 26, Jets 14

The Patriots had looked and looked, but they never could seem to find a pass rush. There were years in which they were sure that elusive pass rush was all that separated them from the playoffs, if not greatness, as in actually winning a playoff game, something they had not done in three tries since 1963.

So it was fitting that their new and improved pass rush helped them to a 26-14 breakthrough victory over the Jets in the first of two weekend wild-card games at Giants Stadium. The Jets realized early that they wouldn't have time to throw deep. They tried only once. Ken O'Brien put it up for Wesley Walker, who was streaking along the sideline, apparently open. But safety Fred Marion had fooled O'Brien. He knew what was coming, broke for the ball at the last instant, and intercepted it inside the Patriots' 10-yard line. Six plays later, Tony Eason's 36-yard bomb to Stanley Morgan against a blitz put New England ahead 13-7.

Now the Patriots' pass rushers could get in their starting blocks. It was the last two minutes of the half. O'Brien had to throw. He had been sacked 62 times, an NFL record, which said two things: The Jets didn't protect him very well, and O'Brien could take it. Not this time, though. From the left side of the New England defense, rookie end Garin Veris scattered the blockers and linebacker Andre Tippett broke into the backfield. His sack left O'Brien with a concussion. O'Brien would not be able to continue past the first possession of the second half.

By then the score was 23-7. Tony Franklin had kicked the third of his four field goals. On the ensuing kickoff, Johnny Rembert stripped the ball from Johnny Hector, picked it up, and ran 15 yards for a touchdown. "That put them in a commanding position," Jets coach Joe Walton said in an understatement.

The Patriots' pass rush had arrived in 1984, when Tippett blossomed as a talented blitzer,

and their sacks increased by one a game to 55. The defense improved in 1985, even though it got six fewer sacks. Tippett led the AFC with 16½ sacks. Veris had 10, tops for an NFL rookie. Veris, who replaced Kenneth Sims when a broken leg ended Sims's best season, had three of New England's five sacks in the victory over the Jets.

"The way Andre Tippett goes about his business is contagious," coach Raymond Berry said. Tippett poured it on against rusty Jets quarterback Pat Ryan, chasing him into Veris and making a sack himself. With 5:20 left, he tipped a pass that was intercepted by Veris. The 18-yard return set up the last field goal.

New England's defense had been teetering midway through the 1984 season. After a 44-24 loss to Miami, coach Ron Meyer fired defensive coordinator Rod Rust. It was not a popular move among players.

"You could call it a revolt," cornerback Raymond Clayborn said. General manager Pat Sullivan, who was attending league meetings, heard the news in a tearful call from his secretary. He hurried home to fire Meyer and hire Berry, who rehired Rust.

"Rod Rust can compete with Don Shula, Bill Walsh, Chuck Noll, Tom Landry, and the other great strategists of the game," Sullivan said.

Rust's flexible 3-4 defense is a melange of alignments and coverages. It brings out the players' best, but Rust resists a genius tag. "All coaching is," he says, "is trying to get them pointed in the right direction."

The Patriots beat the Jets with a 4-0 advantage in turnovers. Those fumble drills, and the pass-receiving drills—for defensive backs—had paid off. The mistake-free offense had just one penalty. Eason completed 12 of 16 passes for 179 yards. Berry said he wasn't surprised to win, "but I still feel numb, frankly. I think I'm operating on batteries."

New York Jets quarterback Ken O'Brien (right) found out that one sack by Patriots Pro Bowl linebacker Andre Tippett can ruin your whole day. With time running out in the first half and the Jets trailing 13-7, O'Brien, who was sacked an NFL-record 62 times during the regular season, was slammed to the turf by Tippett. The result was momentum for New England. . .and a mild concussion for O'Brien. Although he tried, O'Brien couldn't continue past the Jets' first possession of the second half, and was replaced by backup Pat Ryan. In all, New York quarterbacks were sacked five times for 51 yards in losses.

NFC Wild Card

Giants 17, 49ers 3

It was almost a secret, but the New York Giants, not the Bears, led the league in sacks with 68. The Giants had a rowdy, rib-rocking, rip-snorting defense of their own, and they couldn't wait to show it to San Francisco quarterback Joe Montana. Close up.

Montana's pulled rib-cage muscles were hurting badly even before the NFC Wild-Card Game at Giants Stadium. He missed practice on Thursday. But this was Joe Montana, right? Surely he'd find a way to pull off his usual playoff magic, hurting or not.

Looking back, away from the sparkle of the 49ers' Super Bowl rings, it's clear what a mismatch the game was. San Francisco's pass blocking, shaky all season, was missing injured Pro Bowl guard Randy Cross. Center Fred Quillan was playing on an injured knee. If Montana hadn't been hurting before the game, he would have been after it. He took four sacks and countless more blows after throwing the ball, which he had to do 47 times. The 49ers couldn't run. Montana was a bone in a kennel. "I'm not sure we could have beaten them if he was 100 percent," wide receiver Dwight Clark said after the Giants won 17-3.

Montana never had time to test the New York secondary, which had its own injury problems. He had to throw short passes into the heart of the Giants' defense, their linebackers. The receivers took nearly as bad a beating as Montana. They dropped 10 passes. Roger Craig dropped five before reinjuring the knee he had hyperextended two weeks earlier. He left with 23 yards on the ground and 18 in the air. Clark went out early with a concussion.

"That's the best I've ever seen our defense play," Giants quarterback Phil Simms said. "They had the 49ers looking over their shoulders." Even when New York squandered drives throughout the second half, the game never was as close as the score. The 49ers didn't

cross the Giants' 20-yard line until they reached the 13 in the last three minutes.

"You could tell Montana was hurting by the way he would get up off the ground," Giants defensive end Casey Merrill said. "Part by part." Montana went down twice without being touched, just ducking to avoid the blows.

"He was rattled by the way we went after him," defensive end Leonard Marshall said. Marshall led the NFL in sacks much of the year before finishing third with 15. Lawrence Taylor had 13 more of the Giants' 68 sacks and tied for eighth. Inside linebacker Harry Carson joined them on the NFC Pro Bowl team.

So did Simms and Joe Morris. The little running back was the first player in 10 games to run for 100 yards against San Francisco. He ran 28 times for 141 yards and kept the Giants out of passing situations. Simms wasn't sacked.

The Giants had committed themselves to a running game before the season. They hired a new line coach, Fred Hoaglin. They added the "halfback" to what had been a "fullback-oriented" running game. They boosted their rushing attempts by five a game, from thirteenth in the league to second.

Morris's longest run was 30 yards on the second-half drive that put the 49ers out of striking distance after a narrow Giants 10-3 halftime advantage. Simms threw for the last three yards to tight end Don Hasselbeck, who hadn't caught a pass in 15 weeks. He wasn't even the secondary receiver this time.

In the end, it was hard to remember the 49ers had been hailed as a dynasty when they won Super Bowl XIX 11 months earlier. NFL dynasties are like that. They come and go like women's fashions. "You can't always be eighteen-and-one," Montana said. "If you were, it wouldn't be a challenge." San Francisco was the sixth consecutive Super Bowl champion that failed to repeat.

Pint-sized running back Joe Morris (right), all 5 feet 7 inches of him, became a king-sized headache to linebacker Todd Shell (90) and the rest of San Francisco's frustrated defense. Morris upstaged the 49ers' more celebrated Joe—Montana—by rushing for a game-high 141 yards on 28 carries. His 30-yard run in the third quarter set up the Giants' final touchdown, a three-yard pass from Phil Simms to tight end Don Hasselbeck that stretched New York's lead to 17-3.

AFC Divisional Playoff

Dolphins 24, Browns 21

By the end of Don Shula's fifty-sixth birthday, he had to feel 66. His team had its gift list mixed up. The great Miami Dolphins nearly surrendered their first playoff game to the Cleveland Browns, who were merely grateful. Where but in the AFC Central Division could an 8-8 team be champion and be invited to the playoff ball?

"Give them credit," Shula said. Yes, it didn't matter to the Browns that the experts rated them slightly behind the Afghan army. They were taking it to the Dolphins and taking Miami's game away when they jumped on top 21-3 early in the third quarter. But it also was a disturbing reprise in this chewed-up nail of a Miami season. The Dolphins had finished with seven consecutive victories to go 12-4.

"Some days you've got to be shocked before you play well," running back Tony Nathan said. "We've seen this before. We start digging our own graves and then we say, 'Well, it's not time to get in there yet.' "

This time, they climbed out as the dirt was pouring in. "This was as tough a situation as we've been in," Shula said. "If we had lost, it would have been very tough to live with."

But by winning 24-21, the Dolphins looked as dangerous as ever. It was the second-biggest comeback in NFL playoff history. What's more, they made it without their notorious bombs-away offense. They scored three touchdowns in the last 20:13 on nickel-and-dime drives.

Cleveland wasn't giving the deep pass. Its cornerbacks, Frank Minnifield and Hanford Dixon, clobbered the Dolphins' wide receivers at the line, secure in the knowledge that their safeties were waiting behind them. Miami's Marks Brothers—Duper and Clayton—had just one catch all game. Dan Marino was 2 for 7 in the first quarter and threw an end-zone interception in the second. "I wasn't making the right decisions," he said later. "I just had to start being more patient."

Marino had to start settling for shorter passes. Nathan accommodated him with 10 catches, including one that gained 39 yards—mostly running—on the winning touchdown drive. But, before that, Marino heard rare boos in the Orange Bowl.

The Dolphins had gotten themselves into this fine mess by letting Cleveland's backs run all over them for 251 yards. "They like to take a hit," nose tackle Mike Charles said of the Browns' Earnest Byner and Kevin Mack, both of whom had 1,000-yard seasons. "We had three guys hit them and they'd just get up smiling, toss the ball to the ref, and get ready to go again. When you come up against backs like that, you know it's going to be a long day."

Byner, who was in his second season, had a standout day. He gained 161 yards and scored on runs of 21 and 66 yards. The second one, through broken tackles and a broken field, made the score 21-3 early in the second half.

The Dolphins' first touchdown finished a 74-yard drive on 11 pass plays and two runs. It still was the third quarter when rookie Ron Davenport's 31-yard run cut Cleveland's lead to 21-17. But then the Browns toughened. Miami needed a big play from the defense that had been giving them up.

Mack Moore came through. Byner had started to leave the field before a third-and-2 play from Miami's 48, and when he returned to the huddle, he was confused about his blocking assignment. He went the wrong way, and defensive end Moore came free to tackle Curtis Dickey for a six-yard loss.

Nine plays and 73 yards later, Davenport scored from the 1. There was 1:57 to play. Not enough time for the Browns' rookie quarterback Bernie Kosar, who had returned to the scene of college triumphs for the University of Miami. "There's no satisfaction in losing," he said, but the Browns had satisfied their critics.

A relieved Don Shula (right) exchanges congratulations with a disappointed Marty Schottenheimer after Shula's Dolphins scrambled for 21 second-half points to edge Schottenheimer's underdog Browns 24-21 at the Orange Bowl. Trailing 21-3, Miami roared back behind Dan Marino's passes and several key runs, including one for 31 yards and a touchdown by rookie Ron Davenport. When Davenport scored from the 1-yard line with 1:57 to play, the Dolphins had pulled it out. "Great teams don't quit, and they didn't," Browns nose tackle Bob Golic said.

AFC Divisional Playoff

Patriots 27, Raiders 20

After all these years, somebody figured out a way to kick a touchdown. It didn't turn out the way Garo Yepremian had referred to it in 1968, with a kicker just off the boat running out with the field goal team wondering how to fasten his chinstrap. But the wild-card New England Patriots' pet play started with a kickoff and ended with a touchdown. In between, they forced a fumble.

They scored that way for the third week in four when they beat the Los Angeles Raiders 27-20 on the road to advance to the AFC Championship Game. This tide turned in 14 seconds late in the third quarter, changing a 20-17 deficit to a 27-20 lead. Sam Seale of the Raiders dropped a kickoff and picked it up before the Patriots' Mosi Tatupu knocked it loose at the Los Angeles 12-yard line. Rookie safety Jim Bowman fell on it in the end zone for a 24-20 lead.

The Raiders had three more chances to tie, but couldn't get past the Patriots' 41.

The Patriots confiscated the ball a total of six times, losing it only twice for an amazing 10-2 turnover edge in two playoff games. New England had three interceptions and three fumble recoveries against the Raiders. Two of the interceptions set up field goals. New England took a 7-0 lead two plays after a first-quarter variation on their kick-a-touchdown play. This one was a punt. Fulton Walker fumbled and Bowman recovered at the Raiders' 21.

The turnovers helped New England control the ball for 36 minutes 59 seconds. Craig James also helped. No runner had gained 100 yards against the Raiders' defense all season.

"You don't dominate the Raiders," tackle Brian Holloway said. "They're like sharks. They're in a frenzy this time of year. You try to control them."

The Patriots did just that, with James gaining 104 of their 156 rushing yards. The linemen knocked people down. All Tony Eason had to do was avoid interceptions and complete 7 of 14 passes, just one to a wide receiver.

James had four of his 23 carries and 27 yards on the 80-yard drive that kept New England in the game in the second quarter. Marcus Allen, who finished with 121 yards, had just put the Raiders ahead 17-7 with an 11-yard catapult into the end zone.

Now the Patriots drove in nine plays to the Raiders' 2, where Eason called time out. He wanted to make sure no one was pulling his leg. The play that came to the huddle didn't sound like something coach Raymond Berry would call in that situation. It was a running play out of the Shotgun formation.

"I convinced Tony it was my call," Berry said. When he returned to the huddle, Eason announced, "This play's going to score." James cut outside John Hannah's block on the left side to score a touchdown.

Patriots general manager Patrick Sullivan enjoyed the game so much, he couldn't resist rubbing it in. From the Patriots' bench, he taunted Howie Long, the Raiders' all-pro defensive end and a Boston-area native, for much of the second half. After the game, Sullivan caught up with Long on the way to the dressing room. Long faked a punch, and Sullivan yanked his facemask. Raiders linebacker Matt Millen broke them up, and Sullivan wound up with a bandage over his eyebrow.

The Patriots had come a long way from a 2-14 nightmare season in 1981. They had been laughingstocks so long, it was easy to forget about their collection of talent. Eight defensive starters were drafted in the first two rounds. Five first-rounders started on offense.

"They haven't learned how good they can be," Berry had said a few weeks earlier. "They have to get to the point where they know they can win every week. That takes time." But not much, apparently.

New England fullback Mosi Tatupu (right, in white) grimaces as he drags two Raiders, cornerback Lester Hayes (left) and free safety Vann McElroy, with him on a 22-yard run in the second quarter. The drive ended when Craig James scored on a two-yard run to trim the Los Angeles lead to 17-14. The Patriots rushed for a total of 156 yards, with James accounting for 104. It marked the first time any back had gone over 100 yards against the Raiders all season.

NFC Divisional Playoff

Rams 20, Cowboys 0

Eric Dickerson isn't all that hard to spot. He's 6 feet 3 inches, 218 pounds, the guy with goggles. Trouble was, he had become altogether *too* easy to spot. He wasn't his customary blur. Going into the NFC playoff game against Dallas, he had run for 100 yards in only 4 of his last 13 games.

The Cowboys had the treat of welcoming back the Dickerson everyone recognized from his first two seasons, when he ran for 1,808 and 2,105 yards. They welcomed him with open and empty arms. "Eric didn't miss a hole today," guard Dennis Harrah said. "And when there wasn't a hole, he made one."

He broke open the Los Angeles Rams' 20-0 victory at Anaheim Stadium with 248 yards on 34 carries. He had gained just 78 yards by half-time, when the Rams led only 3-0. "All of a sudden it just blew up in our faces," Dallas defensive end Ed (Too Tall) Jones said. "Dickerson just broke down our defense."

To say nothing of the record book. The previous NFL record for a playoff game had been Keith Lincoln's 206 yards for the San Diego Chargers of the AFL in 1963. Dickerson also set the record straight about his relatively disappointing 1,234-yard season, which began with a two-game holdout.

"People were saying I lost the desire, that I wasn't tough, that I couldn't run like I did before," Dickerson said. "But I don't have anything to prove to anybody. I love to play football, and I always give it my best."

Dickerson's 55-yard scoring run on the first play of the second half was his longest of the season. "It's been so long since I've had what I call a home run," he said. He hadn't surpassed his 43-yard gain against Seattle in week 3 when he ended his holdout with 150 yards.

He reached the fences again in the fourth quarter, this time for a 40-yard touchdown. Just as he did on the first score, he burst through desperate hands at the line of scrimmage and outran everyone all the way to the end zone.

The Rams had been shooing away morticians with tape measures for two months. They had won only 4 of 9 games since their 7-0 start. "We're in first place and we stink," Harrah had said after the Saints upset them in week 13. But they stayed in first place.

They had a defense and kicking teams that could win a game if the offense didn't give it away. *Bor-ring*, muttered their media critics. *Win-ning*, was coach John Robinson's answer. The Rams beat Dallas with 47 passing yards, something that may not have happened since footballs had rounded ends. First-year quarterback Dieter Brock completed 6 of 22 passes for 50 yards. With 78 percent of their yardage and both their touchdowns, Dickerson's great game only stoked the fire of the Rams' critics.

"The Rams are eleven-and-five because of their strategy," countered Cowboys coach Tom Landry. "There's nothing more boring than going five-and-eleven."

The kicking teams set up both Los Angeles field goals. Henry Ellard's 23-yard punt return and Vince Newsome's fumble recovery on the kickoff after Dickerson's first touchdown were decisive. The score was 13-0 before Dallas's offense took a snap in the second half.

The game was over.

The Rams play cautious zones instead of attacking like the Bears. "But they both get the job done," Cowboys quarterback Danny White said. He had nowhere to throw. Dallas was shut out for the first time in 36 playoff games.

The Rams had three interceptions, three fumble recoveries, and five sacks, three by reserve sack specialist Gary Jeter. It was their sixth victory without scoring more than 20 points. But for now, the offense looked just fine, wearing his usual number 29. As Robinson said, "There's nothing more exciting than watching that man run."

Eric Dickerson didn't have an "S" emblazoned on his chest, nor was he wearing a cape, it only seemed that way in the Rams' 20-0 victory over Dallas. After shocking the Cowboys with a 55-yard touchdown run on the first play from scrimmage in the third quarter, Dickerson bolted for a 40-yard score early in the fourth period en route to an NFL playoff-record 248 yards. On his second touchdown, Dickerson (right) ran around right end and past Dallas defensive backs Everson Walls (24) and Michael Downs on his way to the end zone. The 248 yards also broke the Rams' single-game rushing record of 247 yards, set by Willie Ellison in 1971.

Bears 21, Giants 0

Buddy Ryan had promised a shutout from his defense. The Bears settled for 21-0 because football doesn't allow negative scores. They made advancing to their second consecutive NFC Championship Game look as simple as crossing items off a shopping list. They held the New York Giants to 67 yards and three first downs before their last two late, meaningless drives.

Just look at Richard Dent, the defensive end who moves blockers around like a kid playing with plastic soldiers. He had 3½ of the six sacks, forced a fumble, knocked down a pass, and stopped three runs in the backfield. His 33 yards on sacks were six more than the Giants' running game gained all day.

The Bears had to stop Joe Morris first. He had run for 142 yards a week earlier against San Francisco. He gained 19 on his first two carries but only 13 on his last 10. They flattened him so thoroughly, linebacker Otis Wilson said, "One time I looked down and I thought it was a poster of him." William Perry delivered the knockout blow, literally, 3½ minutes before half.

"Old-fashioned football," coach Mike Ditka called it, the way they played before helmets and highball glasses were made of plastic, when men were men and grass was grass. Even quarterback Jim McMahon dived into the anti-ballistic Lawrence Taylor for a block. "I think the key still is: Whose line is dominating?" safety Gary Fencik said.

The Bears dominated the same New York lines that had whipped the 49ers thoroughly. They gave no sacks to the NFL leaders, and had the Giants' Phil Simms running for his life. The Smurf version of Ryan's 46 defense substituted safety Shaun Gayle for Perry against three wide receivers. It put Dent over the right guard instead of the right tackle, with linebackers Wilson and Marshall at either end. "They didn't know who to block," Marshall said.

Still, the lead was a shaky 7-0 at halftime. The Bears' only score probably was the shortest punt return in history. Punter Sean Landeta barely ticked the ball and Gayle ran it in from five yards. "I don't know what you'd call it," Gayle said. "A foul tip?"

The Giants had a chance when they began the third quarter with their backs to the wind, but they ended it with their backs to the wall. They had the ball for only two minutes 42 seconds on four possessions. Their 11 plays lost 11 yards. And McMahon's two touchdown passes into the 14-miles-per-hour wind made it 21-0. He credited his sticky batting gloves for the throws of 23 and 20 yards to Dennis McKinnon.

"If my receivers can get used to me throwing spirals for a change, I might use these gloves the rest of my life," McMahon said.

In their final regular-season game, at Detroit, the Bears had tried to shake the dust off their passing game, which had been in storage since October with the lawn chairs and beach balls. It creaked from disuse. But this time, McMahon and Ditka told Willie Gault they were going to need him. His three first-half catches "set the tone early," McMahon said. "The safety played a little bit toward Willie and that's why Dennis was having a heyday."

McKinnon had caught seven touchdown passes in the first eight games, then seven passes total, with no touchdowns, in the next eight. "I thought they'd forgotten me, and I told them so," he said. One reason they neglected him was that he hadn't practiced more than one day a week since his knee surgery on July 5. But in Atlanta for practices, the Bears were back on grass and McKinnon was back on the field.

Besides, it was playoff time. McKinnon had scored the game-winning touchdown against Washington in the 1984 playoffs a month after knee surgery. "This is the time when you show what you are really made of," he said. "This is the time the good teams win."

The New York Giants were the latest challengers to have a thoroughly forgettable day in the Bears' icy lair, Soldier Field. It got downright embarrassing for punter Sean Landeta on one sequence in the first quarter. Punting from his own end zone with the score 0-0, Landeta began his approach to the ball (1). However, after he routinely dropped the ball toward his right foot, Landeta watched the swirling, gusty winds blow the ball off course (2). He was barely able to graze the ball (3), causing it to travel just five yards. When Chicago's Shaun Gayle scooped up the loose ball and took it in from five yards away, the Bears had all the points they would need.

1

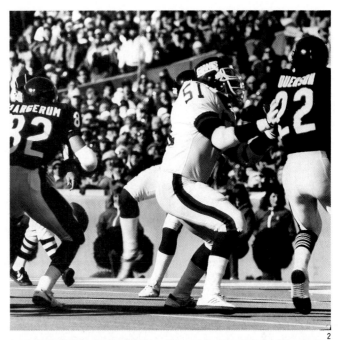

2

3

AFC Championship

Patriots 31, Dolphins 14

The TV camera had caught Miami coach Don Shula smiling as he watched the Patriots finish off the Raiders. He couldn't help it. All that stood between the Dolphins and the Super Bowl was a team that had lost 18 consecutive games in the Orange Bowl by an average margin of 17 points. "We put silver and black gift wrapping on the Patriots for Don Shula," Raiders cornerback Lester Hayes said.

New England's players heard it all. Shula's teams don't turn the ball over. Dan Marino's release nullifies a pass rush. And that great, patient ball control? Forget it. The Dolphins can score in the time it takes to drain the water from an overturned cup.

The Patriots listened. They listened like a 4-year-old who hears all the reasons he can't do something and then says, "But I wanna!" Then they beat Miami 31-14 with ball control, turnovers, and the flip side of a pass rush, punishing pass coverage on the Dolphins' superb wide receivers. Marino was 6 for 24 throwing to them, for 86 yards. Cornerback Raymond Clayborn shut down Mark Duper and intercepted a pass in New England's end zone.

"Our offense never really got into the game," Miami defensive end Doug Betters said. "We were never really threatening, so they never were forced to put the ball up."

So they ran it—59 times for 255 yards. Craig James carried 22 times for 105 and praised coach Raymond Berry for keeping him fresh with alternating backfields. Tony Eason threw only 12 passes, making it a paltry 42 for three playoff games, but he threw zero interceptions in those 42 passes. His 10 completions at Miami included the Patriots' first three touchdowns—4, 1, and 2 yards.

It was the first time a team reached the Super Bowl by winning three road games. The Patriots had been underdogs against all three victims, teams that beat them in the regular season. But Berry's soft-spoken encouragement finally was taking hold. "We were under-achievers," Clayborn said of the pre-Berry Patriots, "but that's all changed."

Even when they were 2-3, Berry said he was proud of them. "He said he enjoyed watching us hustling...and because of that, we kept working," guard John Hannah said.

The Patriots hustled six turnovers from Miami and lost two, going 16-4 for the playoffs. Turnovers set up 24 points, making it 61 of 84 in three weeks.

They started early. New England led 3-0 shortly after Tony Nathan fumbled on the Dolphins' first play. After the teams exchanged touchdown drives, the Patriots cashed in on Marino's fumble on the snap at the Dolphins' 36 and made it 17-7 at halftime.

Then, there it was again. Opening kickoff, second half, Mosi Tatupu knocking the ball loose from Miami's rookie return man Lorenzo Hampton. Six plays later, it was 24-7 after Eason's fourth-and-1 pass to Robert Weathers.

Plenty of time for Marino, though. Early in the fourth quarter, he threw his second touchdown pass right after Roland James lost a fumbled punt at the 10. Uh-oh. James shouldn't even have been returning punts, and this was his second fumble. The Patriots' Irving Fryar, the NFL's leading punt returner, was back home with a cut tendon in his finger. It had been a messy story. Fryar had showed up at the hospital around the same time his bruised wife arrived, the kind of incident that can unravel a dream season.

So it was time to put the Dolphins away. The Patriots did it by pouncing on Joe Carter's fumble, then driving 45 yards on nine consecutive runs to make it 31-14 with 7:34 to play.

"I can't believe it," James said. "I still don't believe it's happened. We're going to the Super Bowl. Wow!"

A three-fingered salute said it all for the amazing New England Patriots. As the final moments of their 31-14 victory over the Dolphins ticked away, the Patriots had accomplished what looked like an impossibility: three consecutive playoff victories, all on the road. Next stop: Bourbon Street.

NFC Championship

Bears 24, Rams 0

The Bears' locker room was quiet. There had been some celebrating on the field, hugging teammates and thrusting fists in the air when the 24-0 victory over the Rams was inevitable. Jim McMahon had stuck his tongue out at a network television camera. Mike Ditka's eyes had misted up when he told the team he'd never seen such dominant defense. But beyond that, winning a trip to the Super Bowl didn't ignite any celebrating. "We'll come up short if we don't win that one," Emery Moorehead said.

Outside the locker room was another matter. Strangers kissed. Horns honked. Grown men barked. Spirits flowed as spirits soared.

The Bears rolled another shutout off the assembly line and washed out two decades of frustration, of the Cubs and White Sox and DePaul teams that lifted Chicago only to drop it head-first before the championship round. It was the first time an NFL team ever had won consecutive playoff shutouts. This time, the Bears' defense outscored the other offense. Wilber Marshall's late 52-yard fumble return even outgained Eric Dickerson. The Rams wound up with 130 yards. They crossed the Chicago 35 only on a fumbled punt.

Someone asked defensive lineman Dan Hampton when the Bears took control of the line of scrimmage. "Kickoff," he said. Maybe even earlier. When the Rams won the toss and chose to receive, safety Gary Fencik clapped. Then he stopped Dickerson for no gain on the first play. The Rams like that weakside run, where the safety is usually off the line. Fencik kept charging up and stuffing it like a turkey.

Dickerson fumbled only twice, instead of the three times that defensive coordinator Buddy Ryan had predicted; Ryan had thought he'd run more than 17 times. Dickerson's 46 yards were 202 behind his output the previous week against Dallas. The Bears took him out of the offense, which was like taking the bow from a violinist.

The end came on third-and-1 with two minutes left in the first quarter and the Bears ahead 10-0. Dickerson broke to the left guard hole. Middle linebacker Mike Singletary got there first. "Mike hit him so hard, I don't think he knew where he was," Marshall said. All day, the linemen handled the blockers, and the linebackers and safeties filled the gaps.

That left the Rams' offense up to quarterback Dieter Brock. Judging from his 10-for-31 passing performance, Brock had a wastebasket in his house with wads of paper lying around it. He passed for 66 yards, never more than 15 on one play. Brock was sacked only three times but the Bears applied suffocating pressure all day.

McMahon *ran* for 16 on the Bears' first touchdown, 5:25 into the game. He had to do something. It was third-and-9. Nobody was open. "I saw an opening," he said. When it closed at the 2, he dived the rest of the way. "That's what makes Jim such a threat," Ditka said.

His other touchdown was a 22-yard pass to Willie Gault in the third quarter. He threw it running to his left with his feet in the air. Ditka hadn't expected him to throw at all. "The coach sent in a draw play I didn't agree with, so I called my own," McMahon said.

"He [McMahon] was a crazy nut out there," Walter Payton said. "He did everything but take his clothes off."

Clothing was the subject of McMahon's most inspired zaniness. Commissioner Pete Rozelle had fined the Bears $5,000 because McMahon and Payton had ignored orders to remove their headbands, which advertised shoe companies. So McMahon wrote ROZELLE on two headbands, gave one to Payton, and took his helmet off at every opportunity. About 20 teammates displayed the logos on their shoes, another league no-no. The Bears were fed up with the powers that be. "When we win the Super Bowl," McMahon said, "they'll have to like us."

For once, Eric Dickerson (29, right) did the chasing as Bears linebacker Wilber Marshall (with ball) headed toward the goal line. Marshall picked up a fourth-quarter fumble by Rams quarterback Dieter Brock and rambled 52 yards for the final points in Chicago's 24-0 victory over the Rams for the NFC championship. The Bears dominated from start to finish, limiting Los Angeles to 130 yards in total offense. Said Bears coach Mike Ditka after the game: "The job won't be complete until we take care of business in New Orleans."

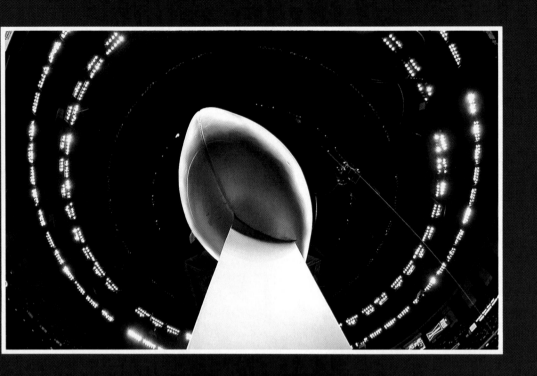

Super Bowl XX

GRIN AND BEAR IT

Super Bowl XX

Bears 46, Patriots 10

The coronation went off without a hitch.

Most people expected the Bears to win the Super Bowl all along. By two, three touchdowns even. But not like this. Not so convincingly that middle linebacker Mike Singletary, with 4:06 left in the first half, would jump up and down in rage, berating his teammates because they had just given up *a first down.*

It was the Patriots' first of the game. It was their eighteenth play, and their third that gained yardage. Their starting quarterback already had been chased from the game. The Bears already had a 20-3 lead.

The Bears just strolled into the Superdome and picked up the Lombardi Trophy as if it were something they'd left at the hat-check counter. They led 44-3 after three quarters, 46-10 at the end. They scored the most points and won the most lopsided victory in all 20 Super Bowls.

The game was decided long before the defensive letdown that ticked off Singletary. Richard Dent saw to that the third and fourth times New England had the ball, when he forced fumbles that his teammates recovered at the Patriots' 13-yard line. The Bears turned them into 10 points and a 13-3 lead, already a rout the way their defense was playing. Dent later was voted most valuable player, just as he had dreamed during the week.

"This is special," coach Mike Ditka said after the formality of the final gun. "We made history today. That's beautiful."

The team that brought us "The Super Bowl Shuffle" played the Patriots like a snare drum. They won in their irrepressible manner of rowdy children, the kind teachers find at once huggable and sluggable, the way they had endeared a nation all year.

Something kept people enthralled. The game set an all-time television record, 127 million viewers, and they weren't staying tuned to see who would win. Fridge Fever no doubt piqued

some curiosity, for which Ditka prescribed William Perry's latest touchdown rumble.

Throughout the game, there was an electrifying sense of *What will they do next?* It was competitive, all right. The Bears' defense was competing with history.

At halftime, the Patriots had one first down, minus-5 yards rushing, minus-14 yards passing, minus-19 yards total—all Super Bowl records. What next? How about a safety and an interception for a touchdown in the second half? The Bears had seven sacks, and it was hard to credit people out of the swarms that enveloped quarterbacks Tony Eason and Steve Grogan. Linebacker Otis Wilson led with two sacks, Dent had 1½. The Bears intercepted two passes and recovered four fumbles.

Chicago held the Patriots to seven rushing yards, another record. The Bears gave up 123 yards total, but they might well have broken the Pittsburgh Steelers' 11-year-old record of 119 if defensive coordinator Buddy Ryan hadn't turned the last 10 minutes over to the F-Troop, his term for the second string. That's when New England gained its last 37 yards.

The Bears' defense dominated the game the way red dominates a fire engine. "I'm not embarrassed, I'm humiliated," Patriots guard Ron Wooten said after it was over.

The Patriots gave it their best shot. They came out passing on their first six plays. "I wanted to get their attention," coach Raymond Berry said. He saw how the Giants' and Rams' ground games had been mauled. The strategy was worth trying. But for the Patriots, who had averaged 14 pass attempts in the playoffs, it was like trying to break a pin with a balloon. "We tried to change the personality of our team in one week," Wooten said. "If we had it to do again, I'd like to see us run right at them."

"It really didn't matter what they did," defensive tackle Steve McMichael said. That was

Singers and dancers of the group Up With People performed their routine during halftime at the Superdome. More than 500 students from 22 countries joined in the celebration.

pretty much the consensus all week. Even then, the matchup stories focused more on Bears versus History than Bears versus Patriots. They certainly had the best defense of the new-rules era, which dawned as Pittsburgh's Steel Curtain started fraying, and drove scoring and passing yards off the old charts.

Dallas coach Tom Landry, who seems to issue superlatives with each passing of Halley's Comet, called the Bears' defense "more dominant than the Steel Curtain."

The Patriots knew about it first-hand. In their 20-7 loss on September 15 in Chicago, they spent 18 seconds in Bears territory. They had six sacks, three interceptions, and 27 rushing yards. The Bears tried to downplay those numbers. From week 6 on, New England's offense had improved by 48 rushing yards and 35 passing yards a game.

But outside the Bears' meeting rooms, who cared? Where Jim McMahon trailed parades of reporters down Bourbon Street, Patriots players might have been getting kicked out of bars all over New Orleans, for all anyone knew. No one would have recognized them.

The week belonged to McMahon. The day-glo quarterback had just the right blend of savvy and flamboyance to hitch his star to the soaring Super Bowl hype like nobody since Joe Namath. The Rozelle headband he wore in the NFC Championship Game would have been enough. Replicas were on sale everywhere. McMahon received hundreds in the mail. But that was getting old. Reporters arrived Monday with blank notebooks. McMahon filled them as the week progressed.

First off, he had a bruised buttock from a hit by the Rams' Doug Reed after he slid feet-first following a sprint-out in the NFC Championship Game. And furthermore, he was hoping to get acupuncture treatments on his sore rear end, but Bears management barred his personal acupuncturist from the team plane. That one

did it. The word for the week was acupuncture. McMahon wrote it on a headband for practice. He also wrote the first name of Hiroshi Shiriashi, the acupuncturist teammate Willie Gault first had befriended while performing on the world track circuit.

By Wednesday morning, Ditka felt compelled to say, "This is not a put-on." He was truly afraid McMahon might miss the game. But Shiriashi was in town. The Illinois State Acupuncture Association had flown him down Tuesday. McMahon had several treatments before Wednesday's practice. "He was two-hundred percent better," Ditka said. The emergency was over.

There was a new one Thursday. This flap dwarfed the scandal of McMahon's mooning a helicopter at practice early in the week. "Just showing them where it hurt," he said. The latest episode supposedly had him calling New Orleans women "sluts" and its men "idiots." A deejay named Boomer said he heard McMahon say this on a Chicago radio station at 6 a.m. in some spaghetti house, so he leaked it to a New Orleans sportscaster friend named Buddy who reported it on television. McMahon denied it with proper indignation and sincerity, and apologies were issued. But not before a few dozen women picketed the Bears' hotel and the television sportscaster was suspended.

The Bears would have filled notebooks without McMahon, from sub linebacker Brian Cabral's free-drink offer to attract reporters (only water, it turned out) to Wilson's setting the record straight that the defenders' barking goes "woof," not "arf." Wilson also said, "I see a big goose egg," and let it slip that he considered the Rams better than the Patriots, a notion some teammates got across more subtly. It didn't set well with the Patriots, naturally.

"They thought we felt superior to them," Gary Fencik said afterward. "I guess now they know why we had reason to believe it."

Walter Payton (right), the Bears' inspirational leader and NFL's all-time leading rusher, fulfilled a dream when he trotted onto the Superdome carpet during the pregame introductions for Super Bowl XX. Said Dan Hampton: "I think Walter's going to be one of those guys you really don't appreciate until he's gone." His teammates, who revere him, and his fans, who cheer him, could only hope that day was far away.

First Quarter

This was not a good start. On the second play of his first Super Bowl, McMahon called a formation that wasn't right for the play. It botched his handoff to Walter Payton just enough for linebacker Don Blackmon to strip the ball. Larry McGrew recovered for the Patriots on Chicago's 19-yard line. New England took a 3-0 lead with only 1:19 gone, the earliest score ever in a Super Bowl.

Ditka had told his team one thing before the game: "Don't let one bad play ruin it." If anything, the fumble showed the Patriots how hopeless it would be. They threw three passes and didn't complete one. They had receivers open. That happens against the Bears. But they dropped one pass, and quarterback Tony Eason wasn't getting time to throw straight.

Payton was pacing the sideline during those three plays, but he needn't have worried. Two more plays and Willie Gault had a 43-yard gain to the Patriots' 26. It was a nice catch, Gault slowing down with Ronnie Lippett's hand in his face. In less than five minutes, it was 3-3.

Eason tried two more passes, both incomplete. On the third-and-10 pass, Wilber Marshall sacked him, with Otis Wilson and Richard Dent close behind. Time to try running the ball. On the next possession, Mike Singletary met Craig James in the left guard hole. No gain. Pass? Oh, no. Here they come. Steve McMichael got there first, so Dent went for the ball. He knocked it from Eason's grasp. Dan Hampton recovered on the 13.

Here, Ditka did an amazing thing. Maybe he thought the game was under control, never mind the scoreboard. But in a 3-3 Super Bowl, on second-and-goal from the 5, he called a halfback pass for William Perry. Yes, Fridge was the I-back. He went in motion, took a pitchout, looked for tight end Emery Moorehead and found only trouble. Moorehead was covered, and linebacker Andre Tippett was bearing

down on Perry. Nose tackle Dennis Owens became the first player to sack a defensive tackle in the Super Bowl.

"That play typifies what we are all about," center Jay Hilgenberg said. "We work very hard, but we have lots of fun." The Bears salvaged a field goal and a 6-3 lead. Besides, Dent was coming back on the field. This time he needed only one play.

"We should have checked out of that play," tackle Brian Holloway said. "You don't run that play with their defense leaning that way." When James tried to circle left end, Dent met him for a five-yard loss and punched the ball away. Singletary recovered at the 13.

So far, the Bears' most effective runner had been fullback Matt Suhey, with gains of five and seven yards. "I was a decoy," said Payton, who attracted crowds everywhere. From the 13, the Bears went to Suhey for two at right guard, then gave him a pitchout to the right side. He burst back behind the pursuit, then went through McGrew at the line of scrimmage and safety Fred Marion at the goal line for an 11-yard touchdown. With 23 seconds left in the first quarter, the Bears led 13-3.

The game was over. The Patriots couldn't pass. They couldn't run. They couldn't even punt. They had tried nine plays without moving forward. James's three-yard run on the last play of the quarter brought their total up to minus-19, but there were no high fives over it. Even Singletary took the indignity unflappably.

The Bears' defense had staked its claim to the line of scrimmage. Their most questionable matchup there was Perry, the rookie, against left guard John Hannah, the perennial all-pro. Ditka had made a big deal of the challenge at the Saturday night meeting. "And Fridge responded," safety Dave Duerson said. "He controlled him all day, and that allowed the linebackers and safeties to flow to the ball."

With the score tied 3-3 and the first quarter nearing an end, the Patriots committed their first of six turnovers when defensive lineman Dan Hampton (right) recovered quarterback Tony Eason's fumble on the New England 13-yard line. Eason was sacked on the play by Richard Dent and Steve McMichael. The Bears' short drive stalled, so Kevin Butler came in and kicked a 24-yard field goal to give Chicago the lead for good, 6-3.

For a minute—the first minute, that is—the Patriots had hope. On the game's second play (far left), Garin Veris, a rookie defensive end who had served as a production assistant for ABC-TV during Super Bowl XIX when he was a student at Stanford, jarred the ball loose from Chicago's Walter Payton. Linebacker Steve Nelson (57) recovered for New England at the Bears' 25-yard line. After an incomplete pass, the Patriots almost got a quick six (left, above) when quarterback Tony Eason threw over the middle to wide receiver Stanley Morgan, heading for the end zone. But the pass was broken up by middle linebacker Mike Singletary (50), and New England settled for a 36-yard field goal and a 3-0 lead two plays later. As the quarter neared its conclusion, the Patriots had the ball at their own 18-yard line when Craig James (left, below) fumbled after colliding with defensive end Richard Dent (95), and Singletary recovered. When Matt Suhey scored two plays later on an 11-yard run, the Bears were in control, 13-3.

Second Quarter

By the time Berry removed Eason from the game, he was 0-for-6 passing with three sacks. In 15 plays, the Patriots had one play that gained forward yardage. They had minus-28 yards passing and minus-8 running. Total: minus-36, or minus-2.4 per play.

"We got to him early and I think he got rattled," Singletary said. "That's when I said, 'Let's go get him.' The look in his eyes said, 'I hope we're not in for another one of these.' "

The Bears went after Eason with their 59 blitz. All three linebackers came, usually Wilson and Marshall from the strongside and Singletary up the middle. There were only enough blockers for two, so Wilson usually came free.

"Eason was bewildered, but it wasn't just him," Duerson said. "It was John Hannah and Brian Holloway and the rest. They weren't sure where they were going because they didn't know what we were doing. We cause havoc."

Even if the Patriots could have handled the Bears man-for-man, they didn't know where to find them. Ryan was mixing up fronts and blitzing schemes. He had said it would help the Patriots to work two weeks on the Bears' defenses. But he also had said, "We're not going to attack them the way we did last time."

That's the key word about the Bears' defense. It attacks. It isn't satisfied just containing an offense. And now that the Patriots had to play catch-up, they had set off what Hampton calls the "Piranha Effect." "When Dent makes a sack, it makes me charge harder," Wilson said.

"It looks like one guy is trying to outdo the other guy, but they're all playing together," Ditka said. One reason the players charge with such abandon is that they know they're going the right place to stop the play. Ryan wouldn't send them anywhere else.

"There are some defenses that stop a formation and there are some that won't," McMichael said. "Buddy Ryan puts us in the defense that will stop the formation."

Eason knew that. "I tried to scramble, but there was no place to go," he said. "They played an almost perfect game."

After James's gain finished the first quarter, there was an incomplete pass and Hampton's tackle for a four-yard loss. On the next possession, Dent stopped a run at the line, Marshall stopped one for minus-two, and McMichael chased Eason into Wilson for a sack.

The Bears were having fun already. They had gone ahead 20-3 on a 59-yard drive that ended with McMahon's two-yard run, 7:24 before halftime. The scoring play was a college-style triple option. McMahon faked to Perry at fullback, then followed blocks by Perry and tight end Tim Wrightman instead of pitching to Payton.

The fun backfired after Wilson's sack. The Bears tried a reverse on a punt return, even with good field position assured on the punt from the 16. Cornerback Leslie Frazier injured his knee on the play. "It shouldn't have happened," Ditka said, but Frazier needed reconstructive surgery and is unlikely to play in the 1986 season.

Two plays later, Suhey lost a fumble, and Grogan replaced Eason with 5:08 left. The Patriots drove just far enough to infuriate Singletary before they punted, and the Bears responded with a two-minute drive that made it 23-3 at halftime. Kevin Butler kicked his third field goal with three seconds remaining.

It shouldn't have counted, league officials said later. To beat the clock, Hilgenberg had snapped the ball before the offense was set; thus, the half should have ended on an offensive penalty. But they couldn't take points off the scoreboard. Nearly the entire stadium of fans —all except the Patriots' diehards—was stomping and singing the Bears' song. *"We're not here to start no trouble. We're just here to do the Super Bowl Shuffle."*

Tony Eason wasn't dreaming on Super Sunday. That band of angry Bears really did seem permanently attached to his back. Eason got his first taste of just how painful a day it would be on the Patriots' second possession when, facing third-and-10 from his own 41, he was buried (right) by blitzing linebackers Wilber Marshall and Otis Wilson (55). When it was over, the Bears had tied a Super Bowl record for most sacks in one game, with seven.

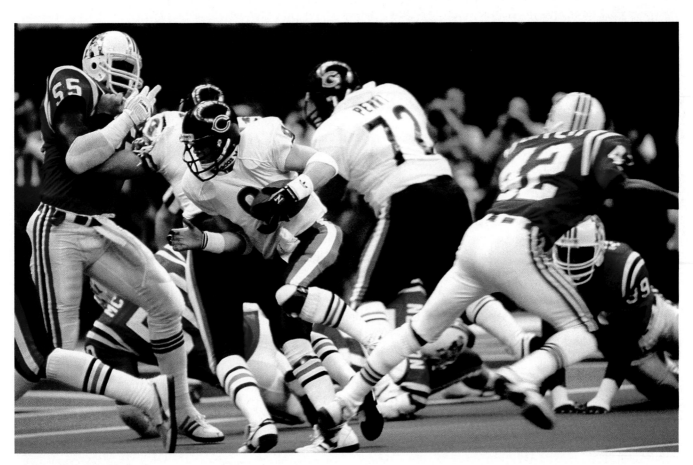

Wherever he went during Super Bowl week, Jim McMahon was the center of attention. From his own 40-yard line late in the first half, McMahon (left) threw a pass toward the right sideline that was deflected by the Patriots' active outside linebacker, Andre Tippett (56), and fell incomplete. Undaunted, McMahon drove the Bears to a field goal. Earlier in the quarter, McMahon scored the first of his two touchdowns (above), running two yards to give Chicago a commanding 20-3 lead. Helping to clear the way for McMahon was William (The Refrigerator) Perry (72). Said coach Mike Ditka of McMahon: "I love him. He's got the guts of a burglar."

Second Half

The points just kept on coming. The Bears' first play of the second half started at their own 4 after Rich Camarillo's 62-yard punt. The play went 60 yards. Gault, whose four catches gained 129 yards, caught the ball at the 50 and would have had a 96-yard touchdown if he hadn't had to slow down for the ball. As it was, McMahon scored from one foot.

Grogan had been picking on Reggie Phillips, the rookie who replaced Frazier. Now it was Phillips's turn. When Marshall tipped a pass, Phillips caught it at the Patriots' 28 and ran in for a 37-3 lead with 6:16 left in the third quarter. He was the twenty-fourth Bear and eleventh defensive player, counting Perry, to score in the season. Rookie linebacker Jim Morrissey almost made it 25 and 12 after the F-Troop got in, but his 47-yard interception return ended at the 5.

"A lot of people have tuned in just to watch our defense," Hampton said. "They say, 'I hope their offense punts.'" But the defense didn't stay on the field long. Two plays after Phillips's touchdown, Fencik jarred the ball from Stanley Morgan and Marshall recovered at the 31. With 3:22 to go in the quarter, it was 44-3.

That was Perry's touchdown, a simple one-man stampede over left guard. It was the Bears' fourth on the ground, a Super Bowl record. Their 21-point quarter tied a record. But these were the Bears, remember. Time for a controversy. Why, in the name of 11 years and the Hall of Fame, didn't the touchdown go to Payton?

"I don't think we used Walter as much as we should have or could have," McMahon said. "I felt bad for him." Payton said he was "surprised" and "disappointed" about not scoring. His 22 carries gained 61 yards.

New England's touchdown came with 13:14 to play. The 76-yard drive included seven of the Patriots' 12 first downs. The fourth-and-8 scoring pass from Grogan to Irving Fryar was a nice touch. The two had been big reasons for New England's success all year, but injuries had made their availability for the Super Bowl uncertain.

McMahon already was out of the game. His 12-for-20 passing had gained 256 yards without an interception. He ran for two touchdowns and finished second in the MVP voting.

He had dedicated the game to Dan Plater, his former college receiver whose career ended with a brain tumor. Plater's nickname, Pluto, was on one of McMahon's headbands. Others advertised research for juvenile diabetes, children's hospital, and POWs and MIAs.

Henry Waechter finished the scoring when he sacked Grogan for a safety with 5:36 to go. Now it was perfect. The team that made 46 a synonym for revolutionary defense would win the Super Bowl with 46 points. It also precisely doubled the score that had driven them here, the 23-0 loss at San Francisco in the 1984 NFC Championship Game.

"I wanted to forget that game so much," Hampton said, "but you really can't when you wake up in the middle of the night and see that score on the scoreboard."

For three games, against the best the NFL could offer, the Bears' defense had allowed an average of 144.7 yards and 10.7 first downs. The averages through three quarters, before meaningless yardage time, were more astounding: 70.0 yards and 3.7 first downs. The defense had given up first downs on only 16 of its opponents' 44 possessions. It had held teams to just three successes in 36 third-down opportunities and 23 minutes a game of possession time. Chicago had 16 sacks, three interceptions, and seven fumble recoveries. It outscored the other teams 91-10.

"We're the best of all time," Duerson said.

But let's ask the harshest critic. Singletary had rated the defense an 8½ against the Giants, 9½ against the Rams. What now? "As close to a ten as we've had all year," he said. "I feel like I could jump on top of the Superdome."

What faint hopes the Patriots still had when the second half began evaporated as fast as Willie Gault can run. Passing from his own end zone on first down after a New England punt, Bears quarterback Jim McMahon faked handoffs to his two running backs, Matt Suhey and Walter Payton, then threw long to Gault (right), who caught the ball behind free safety Fred Marion as he was streaking toward the right sideline. The play covered 60 yards. Eight plays later, McMahon finished things off with a one-yard touchdown run as the Bears took an insurmountable 30-3 lead.

When cornerback Leslie Frazier severely injured a knee in the second quarter, it didn't slow the Bears. Reggie Phillips (48), a rookie from SMU, replaced Frazier and returned an intercepted pass 28 yards for a third-quarter touchdown (top, left) that gave Chicago a 37-3 lead. Three plays later, New England's Craig James fumbled after catching a 14-yard pass. Linebacker Wilber Marshall (58) picked up the ball (bottom, left) and returned it 10 yards to the Patriots' 40, before lateraling to Otis Wilson for three more yards. William Perry (below) finished the Bears' final scoring drive by crashing into linebacker Larry McGrew on a one-yard touchdown run.

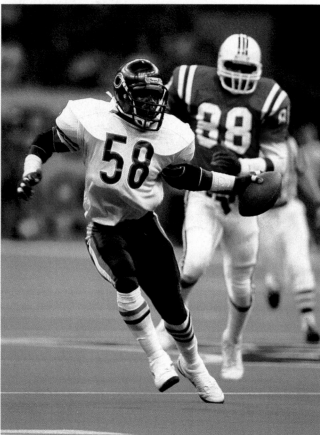

Aftermath

In the last two minutes, the defensive starters surrounded president Mike McCaskey on the sideline. They begged him to do whatever it took to keep Ryan from becoming someone else's head coach. "We got the corporate answer," Duerson said. The players' response was to carry Ryan off the field.

Hampton was the players' spokesman. He said they would be a good defense without Ryan. With Ryan, he said, they would go to the Super Bowl the next five years. The players believed it. They repeatedly called him the MVP of the defense.

"Buddy puts you in position where you can play your best," Wilson said. "He talks to you. If you have problems, he'll sit and listen to you. He can relate to you. He's our inspiration, he's a genius, he's our enemy, he's our friend. He's everything."

The players had an idea he was leaving after their meeting Saturday night. Ryan told them he was proud of the way they had fought back to be the best defense. Then, with tears showing on his cheeks, he said, "Whatever happens, I want you to know you're my heroes." McMichael picked up a chair and threw it through the blackboard. Hampton knocked a reel off the film projector. End of meeting.

"It was like your father telling you, 'I've got to go somewhere else, but you're still my son,'" Singletary said. "It was like watching your family break up."

"We love each other," McMichael said. "That's why we play so good."

Ryan took the Eagles' head coaching job two days later. As Ditka pointed out, the players were staying. The Bears still had a great defense. Aggressive? The Bears played aggressive defense before Ryan played football. Didn't they inherit a classic nickname? The Monsters of the Midway were back.

The usual question came up, and Ditka answered, "I don't believe in the word 'dynasty.'" He said time was the test of true champions. As with every game, the Bears would take their Super Bowls one at a time.

The future looked bright. They had the NFC's youngest team. All but two defensive starters were rookies in the '80s. They had won the Super Bowl without leaning on Payton. They had won 34 of their last 42 games. They had beaten the NFC's five 10-game winners in 1985 by a combined 160-20.

But nothing was guaranteed. Money could be a problem. McCaskey was leading the NFL's charge toward fiscal responsibility, and the cost had been year-long holdouts by starters Todd Bell and Al Harris. Now Dent was threatening to do the same, and nine others had contracts on the verge of expiring.

Chicago didn't care. Next year? After 23 years, next year finally had arrived. The city had its first major sports champion since the Bears won the NFL title in 1963. Its big shoulders had slumped under snow-belt recession, but now they were broad with pride.

"I always felt Chicago was a Bear town," Ditka said. "But I think people had trouble getting it out of their throats for twenty-two years."

Sunday night, inbound expressways had two-mile gridlock from fans driving downtown to share in the celebration. There were 500,000 on the six-block route for Monday's ticker-tape parade. Another 150,000 saw the reception at the Daley Plaza civic center, renamed Bears Plaza for the day. The mayor mentioned a street he wanted to rename George S. Halas Drive.

Several weeks earlier, Singletary had stressed the importance of not letting up. He didn't want people remembering the 1985 Bears and saying, "Well, they were a pretty good team." He wanted them to say, "They were the best. Not just of 1985. The best of all-time." Right now, no one was arguing.

As the game wore on, the Patriots' deficit continued to spiral out of control. With the suspense gone since the first quarter, and the outcome determined not long after—or so it seemed—New England players (right) looked to their lone remaining ally, the clock, for relief.

To the victors go the smiles. . .and for Richard Dent (right), once a little-known eighth-round draft choice, the day truly was extraordinary: two forced fumbles, 1½ sacks, non-stop havoc, and the game's most valuable player award. Everyone, it seemed, got in on the fun for Chicago, including rookie linebacker Jim Morrissey (51, below), who intercepted Steve Grogan's pass at the Bears' 48-yard line and returned it to the New England 5. Words hardly were necessary when Jim McMahon and Walter Payton embraced (right). Payton had reached the summit at last.

Appendix

CHICAGO BEARS 1986

EDWARD W. McCASKEY
Chairman of the Board

MICHAEL B. McCASKEY
President-CEO

VIRGINIA H. McCASKEY
Secretary

JERRY VAINISI
V.P.-General Manager

MIKE DITKA
Head Coach

4 STEVE FULLER
Quarterback

6 KEVIN BUTLER
Kicker

8 MAURY BUFORD
Punter

9 JIM McMAHON
Quarterback

18 MIKE TOMCZAK
Quarterback

20 THOMAS SANDERS
Running Back

21 LESLIE FRAZIER
Cornerback

22 DAVE DUERSON
Safety

23 SHAUN GAYLE
Cornerback

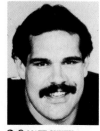
26 MATT SUHEY
Running Back

27 M. RICHARDSON
Cornerback

29 DENNIS GENTRY
Running Back

31 KEN TAYLOR
Cornerback

33 CALVIN THOMAS
Running Back

34 WALTER PAYTON
Running Back

45 GARY FENCIK
Safety

48 REGGIE PHILLIPS
Cornerback

50 MIKE SINGLETARY
Linebacker

51 JIM MORRISSEY
Linebacker

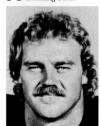
52 CLIFF THRIFT
Linebacker

54 BRIAN CABRAL
Linebacker

55 OTIS WILSON
Linebacker

57 TOM THAYER
Guard-Center

58 W. MARSHALL
Linebacker

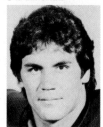
59 RON RIVERA
Linebacker

60 TOM ANDREWS
Center

62 MARK BORTZ
Guard

63 JAY HILGENBERG
Center

70 HENRY WAECHTER
Defensive Tackle

71 ANDY FREDERICK
Tackle

72 WILLIAM PERRY
Defensive Tackle

73 M. HARTENSTINE
Defensive End

74 JIM COVERT
Tackle

75 S. HUMPHRIES
Guard

76 STEVE McMICHAEL
Defensive Tackle

78 KEITH VAN HORNE
Tackle

80 TIM WRIGHTMAN
Tight End

82 KEN MARGERUM
Wide Receiver

83 WILLIE GAULT
Wide Receiver

85 DENNIS McKINNON
Wide Receiver

87 E. MOOREHEAD
Tight End

89 KEITH ORTEGO
Wide Receiver

95 RICHARD DENT
Defensive End

98 TYRONE KEYS
Defensive End

99 DAN HAMPTON
Defensive Tackle

DALE HAUPT
Assistant Coach

ED HUGHES
Assistant Coach

STEVE KAZOR
Assistant Coach

JIM LaRUE
Assistant Coach

TED PLUMB
Assistant Coach

JOHNNY ROLAND
Assistant Coach

BUDDY RYAN
Assistant Coach

DICK STANFEL
Assistant Coach

BILL TOBIN
Dir. of Player Personnel

BILL McGRANE
Dir. of Communications

PAT McCASKEY
Community Involvement

KEN VALDISERRI
Dir. of Media Relations

FRED CAITO
Trainer

RAY EARLEY
Equipment Manager

CLYDE EMRICH
Strength Coordinator

MITCH FRIEDMAN
Photographic Services

ALPHABETICAL ROSTER

No.	Name	Pos.	Ht.	Wt.	Birthdate	NFL Exp.	College
60	Andrews, Tom	C	6-4	267	1/21/61	2	Louisville
62	Bortz, Mark	G	6-6	269	2/12/61	3	Iowa
8	Buford, Maury	P	6-1	191	2/18/60	4	Texas Tech
6	Butler, Kevin	K	6-1	204	7/24/62	R	Georgia
54	Cabral, Brian	LB	6-1	224	6/23/56	7	Colorado
74	Covert, Jim	T	6-4	271	3/22/60	3	Pittsburgh
95	Dent, Richard	DE	6-5	263	12/13/60	3	Tennessee State
22	Duerson, Dave	S	6-1	203	11/28/60	3	Notre Dame
45	Fencik, Gary	S	6-1	196	6/11/54	10	Yale
21	Frazier, Leslie	CB	6-0	187	4/3/59	5	Alcorn State
71	Frederick, Andy	T	6-6	265	7/25/54	9	New Mexico
4	Fuller, Steve	QB	6-4	195	1/5/57	7	Clemson
83	Gault, Willie	WR	6-1	183	9/5/60	3	Tennessee
23	Gayle, Shaun	CB	5-11	193	3/8/62	2	Ohio State
29	Gentry, Dennis	RB	5-8	181	2/10/59	4	Baylor
99	Hampton, Dan	DE-DT	6-5	267	9/19/57	7	Arkansas
73	Hartenstine, Mike	DE	6-3	254	7/27/53	11	Penn State
63	Hilgenberg, Jay	C	6-3	258	3/21/59	5	Iowa
75	Humphries, Stefan	G	6-3	263	1/20/62	2	Michigan
98	Keys, Tyrone	DE	6-7	267	10/24/59	3	Mississippi State
82	Margerum, Ken	WR	6-0	180	10/5/58	4	Stanford
58	Marshall, Wilber	LB	6-1	225	4/18/62	2	Florida
85	McKinnon, Dennis	WR	6-1	185	8/22/61	3	Florida State
9	McMahon, Jim	QB	6-1	190	8/21/59	4	BYU
76	McMichael, Steve	DT	6-2	260	10/17/57	6	Texas
87	Moorehead, Emery	TE	6-2	220	3/22/54	9	Colorado
51	Morrissey, Jim	LB	6-3	215	12/24/62	R	Michigan State
89	Ortego, Keith	WR	6-0	180	8/30/63	R	McNeese State
34	Payton, Walter	RB	5-10	202	7/25/54	11	Jackson State
72	Perry, William	DT	6-2	308	12/16/62	R	Clemson
48	Phillips, Reggie	CB	5-10	170	12/12/60	R	SMU
27	Richardson, Mike	CB	6-0	188	5/23/61	3	Arizona State
59	Rivera, Ron	LB	6-3	239	1/7/62	2	California
20	Sanders, Thomas	RB	5-11	203	1/4/62	R	Texas A&M
50	Singletary, Mike	LB	6-0	228	10/9/58	5	Baylor
26	Suhey, Matt	RB	5-11	216	7/7/58	6	Penn State
31	Taylor, Ken	CB	6-1	185	9/2/63	R	Oregon State
57	Thayer, Tom	G-C	6-4	261	8/16/61	R	Notre Dame
33	Thomas, Calvin	RB	5-11	245	1/7/60	4	Illinois
52	Thrift, Cliff	LB	6-1	230	5/3/56	7	East Central Oklahoma
18	Tomczak, Mike	QB	6-1	195	10/23/62	R	Ohio State
78	Van Horne, Keith	T	6-6	280	11/6/57	5	USC
70	Waechter, Henry	DT	6-5	275	2/13/59	4	Nebraska
55	Wilson, Otis	LB	6-2	232	9/15/57	6	Louisville
80	Wrightman, Tim	TE	6-3	237	3/27/60	R	UCLA

R—A first-year player who has not previously been in an NFL training camp.

GAME BY GAME: BEARS

Bears 38, Tampa Bay 28

at Soldier Field—September 8

Tampa Bay	14	14	0	0	— 28
Bears	7	10	14	7	— 38

BUCS—Magee 1 pass from DeBerg (Igwebuike kick); BEARS—McKinnon 21 pass from McMahon (Butler kick); BUCS—House 44 pass from DeBerg (Igwebuike kick); BUCS—J. Bell 11 pass from DeBerg (Igwebuike kick); BEARS—McMahon 1 run (Butler kick); BEARS—FG Butler 38; BUCS—Wilder 3 run (Igwebuike kick); BEARS—Frazier 29 interception return (Butler kick); BEARS— Suhey 9 pass from McMahon (Butler kick); BEARS—McMahon 1 run (Butler kick).

TEAM STATISTICS

	Bears	Bucs
First Downs	27	17
Total Net Yards	436	307
Net Yards Rushing	185	166
Net Yards Passing	251	141
Passes (Att/Comp/Int)	34-23-1	21-13-2
Punts Average	2-57.5	6-36.8
Fumbles Lost	2-2	0-0
Penalties-Yards	8-78	12-80

INDIVIDUAL STATISTICS

Rushing

BEARS—Payton 17-120; Suhey 8-27; Thomas 3-12; McMahon 4-18; Gentry 2-8.

BUCS—Wilder 27-166, 1 TD; DeBerg 2-0.

Passing

BEARS—McMahon 23-34, 274, 2 TDs.

BUCS—DeBerg 13-21, 160, 3 TDs.

Receiving

BEARS—Payton 6-37; Gault 4-60; McKinnon 4-58; Wrightman 1-27; Thomas 3-32; Moorehead 2-31; Margerum 2-20; Suhey 1-9.

BUCS—Wilder 1-5; Giles 1-18; J. Bell 6-74; Magee 1-1; House 1-44; Carter 3-18.

Bears 20, Patriots 7

at Soldier Field—September 15

Patriots	0	0	0	7	— 7
Bears	7	3	10	0	— 20

BEARS—McKinnon 32 pass from McMahon (Butler kick); BEARS—FG Butler 21; BEARS—Suhey 1 run (Butler kick); BEARS—FG Butler 28; PATRIOTS—C. James 90 pass from Eason.

TEAM STATISTICS

	Bears	Patriots
First Downs	18	10
Total Net Yards	369	206
Net Yards Rushing	160	27
Net Yards Passing	209	179
Passes (Att/Comp/Int)	23-13-1	35-15-3
Punts Average	8-37.4	11-46.7
Fumbles Lost	1-1	1-1
Penalties-Yards	2-10	8-70

INDIVIDUAL STATISTICS

Rushing

BEARS—Payton 11-39; Suhey 9-36; McKinnon 1-0; Thomas 5-22; McMahon 3-8; Gentry 4-10; Sanders 10-37; Fuller 1-8.

PATRIOTS—Collins 7-19; C. James 5-7; Weathers 2-3.

Passing

BEARS—McMahon 13-21, 232, 1 TD; Payton 0-1, Fuller 0-1.

PATRIOTS—Eason 15-35, 234, 1 TD.

Receiving

BEARS—Payton 1-1; McKinnon 5-73; Moorehead 2-25; Margerum 2-16; Wrightman 2-74; Gault 1-43.

PATRIOTS—D. Williams 3-46; Ramsey 5-51; Jones 2-26; Collins 3-16; Morgan 1-5; C. James 1-90.

Bears 33, Minnesota 24

at Metrodome—September 19

Bears	3	3	24	3	— 33
Vikings	3	7	7	7	— 24

BEARS—FG Butler 24; MINN—FG Stenerud 25; BEARS—FG Butler 19; MINN—Carter 14 pass from Kramer (Stenerud kick); BEARS—FG Butler 34; MINN—Jones 9 pass from Kramer (Stenerud kick); BEARS—Gault 70 pass from McMahon (Butler kick); BEARS—McKinnon 25 pass from McMahon (Butler kick); BEARS—McKinnon 43 pass from McMahon (Butler kick); MINN—Carter 57 pass from Kramer (Stenerud kick); BEARS—FG Butler 31.

TEAM STATISTICS

	Bears	Minn
First Downs	21	23
Total Net Yards	480	445
Net Yards Rushing	127	34
Net Yards Passing	353	411
Passes (Att/Comp/Int)	33-21-1	55-28-3
Punts Average	3-40	3-43.3
Fumbles Lost	0-0	3-2
Penalties-Yards	10-66	6-45

INDIVIDUAL STATISTICS

Rushing

BEARS—Payton 15-62; Fuller 2-4; Suhey 8-41; Thomas 1-2; McMahon 4-18.

MINN—Anderson 7-10; Nelson 5-18; Brown 1-6; Coleman 2-0.

Passing

BEARS—Fuller 13-18, 124; McMahon 8-15, 236, 3 TDs.

MINN—Kramer 28-55, 436, 3 TDs.

Receiving

BEARS—Payton 5-17; Gault 5-146; Moorehead 1-13; Wrightman 1-5; Suhey 1-21; Anderson 1-6; McKinnon 4-133; Margerum 2-19.

MINN—Jordan 5-66; Nelson 2-10; Jones 4-43; Carter 4-102; Mularkey 2-26; Rhymes 3-89; Rice 1-11; Anderson 2-14; Brown 1-9; Lewis 4-66.

Bears 45, Redskins 10

at Soldier Field—September 29

Redskins	7	3	0	0	— 10
Bears	0	31	7	7	— 45

REDSKINS—Riggins 7 run (Moseley kick); REDSKINS—FG Moseley 32; BEARS—Gault 99 kickoff return (Butler kick); BEARS—McKinnon 14 pass from McMahon (Butler kick); BEARS—Moorehead 10 pass from McMahon (Butler kick); BEARS—McMahon 13 pass from Payton (Butler kick); BEARS—FG Butler 28; BEARS—Payton 33 pass from McMahon (Butler kick); BEARS—Gentry 1 run (Butler kick).

TEAM STATISTICS

	Bears	Redskins
First Downs	16	19
Total Net Yards	250	376
Net Yards Rushing	91	192
Net Yards Passing	159	184
Passes (Att/Comp/Int)	21-14-1	39-21-2
Punts Average	5-41.4	5-26.6
Fumbles Lost	0-0	1-1
Penalties-Yards	6-50	10-85

INDIVIDUAL STATISTICS

Rushing

BEARS—Payton 7-6; Suhey 5-14; Thomas 1-1; McMahon 3-36; Gentry 2-(−1); Fuller 1-0; Sanders 3-35.

REDSKINS—Riggins 11-29; Theismann 4-7; Rogers 13-80; Wonsley 1-0; Griffin 4-37; Jenkins 2-39.

Passing

BEARS—McMahon 13-19, 160, 3 TDs; Payton 1-1, 13, 1 TD; Fuller 0-1.

REDSKINS—Theismann 21-39, 209.

Receiving

BEARS—McKinnon 3-50; Thomas 1-6; Moorehead 3-34; Suhey 3-11; McMahon 1-13; Payton 2-41; Margerum 1-18.

REDSKINS—Didier 8-92; Clark 5-76; Monk 4-14; Giffin 2-7; Muhammed 1-8; Warren 1-12.

Bears 27, Tampa Bay 19

at Tampa Stadium—October 6

Bears	0	3	10	14	— 27
Tampa Bay	0	12	0	7	— 19

BUCS—FG Igwebuike 19; BUCS—House 21 pass from DeBerg (kick failed); BUCS—FG Igwebuike 36; BEARS—FG Butler 30; BEARS—McKinnon 21 pass from McMahon (Butler kick); BEARS—FG Butler 30; BEARS—Payton 4 run (Butler kick); BUCS—Carter 25 pass from DeBerg (Igwebuike kick); BEARS—Payton 9 run (Butler kick).

TEAM STATISTICS

	Bears	Bucs
First Downs	22	19
Total Net Yards	433	373
Net Yards Rushing	147	27
Net Yards Passing	286	346
Passes (Att/Comp/Int)	34-22-2	43-23-2
Punts Average	4-54.0	4-44.5
Fumbles Lost	2-1	3-1
Penalties-Yards	9-67	5-40

INDIVIDUAL STATISTICS

Rushing

BEARS—Suhey 6-38; Gault 1-(−3); Payton 16-63; McMahon 8-46; Thomas 1-3.

BUCS—Wilder 18-29; Springs 1-(−2); DeBerg 1-0.

Passing

BEARS—McMahon 22-34, 292, 1 TD.

BUCS—DeBerg 23-43, 346, 2 TDs.

Receiving

BEARS—Payton 1-9; Moorehead 8-114; Margerum 1-9; Thomas 1-7; Suhey 5-30; McKinnon 4-67; Gault 2-56.

BUCS—Wilder 4-31; Carter 2-46; Giles 7-112; House 6-100; J. Bell 3-50; Magee 1-7.

Bears 26, 49ers 10

at Candlestick Park—October 13

Bears	13	3	0	10	— 26
49ers	0	10	0	0	— 10

BEARS—Payton 3 run (Butler kick); BEARS—FG Butler 34; BEARS—FG Butler 38; BEARS—FG Butler 27; 49ERS—Williamson 43 interception return (Wersching kick); 49ERS—FG Wersching 32; BEARS—FG Butler 29; BEARS—Payton 17 run (Butler kick).

TEAM STATISTICS

	Bears	49ers
First Downs	22	11
Total Net Yards	372	183
Net Yards Rushing	189	67
Net Yards Passing	183	116
Passes (Att/Comp/Int)	31-8-1	29-17-0
Punts Average	3-45.0	7-47.6
Fumbles Lost	1-0	4-2
Penalties-Yards	7-45	13-94

INDIVIDUAL STATISTICS

Rushing

BEARS—Payton 24-132; McMahon 4-24; Suhey 6-22; Gault 1-5; Perry 2-4; Gentry 1-3; Sanders 1-(−1).

49ERS—Craig 4-42; Tyler 6-25; Montana 2-0.

Passing

BEARS—McMahon 18-31, 186.

49ERS—Montana 17-29, 160.

Receiving

BEARS—Payton 5-34; Suhey 5-25; Wrightman 3-56; Gault 3-50; Margerum 2-21.

49ERS—Clark 4-41; Tyler 4-36; Rice 3-37; Ring 2-14; Francis 2-13; Craig 1-14; Harmon 1-5.

Bears 23, Green Bay Packers 7

at Soldier Field—October 21

Green Bay Packers	7	0	0	0	— 7
Bears	0	21	0	2	— 23

PACKERS—Lofton 27 pass from Dickey (Del Greco kick); BEARS—Payton 2 run (Butler kick); BEARS—Perry 1 run (Butler kick); BEARS—Payton 1 run (Butler kick); BEARS—Wilson sacked Zorn in end zone.

TEAM STATISTICS

	Bears	Packers
First Downs	24	16
Total Net Yards	342	319
Net Yards Rushing	175	96
Net Yards Passing	167	223
Passes (Att/Comp/Int)	32-15-0	31-14-4
Punts Average	5-54.6	6-39.7
Fumbles Lost	7-4	2-1
Penalties-Yards	6-45	10-70

INDIVIDUAL STATISTICS

Rushing

BEARS—Payton 25-112; Suhey 7-31; McMahon 4-27; Perry 1-1; Gentry 1-5; Tomczak 1-0; Fuller 2-(−1).

PACKERS—Clark 14-50; Ivery 7-25; Dickey 1-3; Wright 1-8; Ellis 3-10.

Passing

BEARS—McMahon 12-26, 144; Buford 1-5, 5; Fuller 2-5, 23.

PACKERS—Dickey 4-7, 62, 1 TD; Wright 9-22, 179; Zorn 1-2, 9.

Receiving

BEARS—Suhey 3-33; Payton 4-41; McKinnon 3-40; Gault 2-18; Moorehead 2-28; Wrightman 1-12.

PACKERS—Epps 3-59; Lofton 7-103; Coffman 2-52; Clark 1-27; Ivery 1-9.

Bears 27, Minnesota 9

at Soldier Field—October 27

Minnesota	0	7	0	2	— 9
Bears	10	3	7	7	— 27

BEARS—McKinnon 33 pass from McMahon (Butler kick); BEARS—FG Butler 40; MINN—Nelson 1 run (Stenerud kick); BEARS—FG Butler 29; BEARS—Wilson 23 interception return (Butler kick); BEARS—Payton 20 pass from McMahon (Butler kick); MINN—Elshire safety, tackled Fuller in end zone.

TEAM STATISTICS

	Bears	Minn
First Downs	24	16
Total Net Yards	413	236
Net Yards Rushing	202	30
Net Yards Passing	211	206
Passes (Att/Comp/Int)	34-19-1	46-21-5
Punts Average	4-47.0	6-42.0
Fumbles Lost	1-1	0-0
Penalties-Yards	6-77	8-60

INDIVIDUAL STATISTICS

Rushing

BEARS—Payton 19-118; Suhey 10-34; Gault 1-5; McMahon 1-8; Sanders 4-6; Gentry 4-31.

MINN—Anderson 4-8; Nelson 8-22; Kramer 1-(−1); Rice 1-1.

Passing

BEARS—McMahon 18-31, 181, 2 TDs; Fuller 1-3, 34.

MINN—Kramer 16-33, 176; Wilson 5-13, 60.

Receiving

BEARS—Payton 5-37; Moorehead 4-53; McKinnon 1-33; Suhey 5-38; Gault 1-7; Wrightman 2-13; Manness 1-34.

MINN—Jordan 5-35; Nelson 5-44; Carter 2-32; Lewis 4-79; Anderson 3-21; Mularkey 1-12; Jones 1-13.

Bears 16, Green Bay Packers 10

at Lambeau Field—November 3

Bears	0	7	0	9	— 16
Packers	3	0	7	0	— 10

PACKERS—FG Del Greco 40; BEARS—Perry 4 pass from McMahon (Butler kick); PACKERS—Clark 55 pass from Zorn (Del Greco kick); BEARS—Safety McMichael tackled Zorn in end zone; BEARS—Payton 27 run (Butler kick).

TEAM STATISTICS

	Bears	Packers
First Downs	16	15
Total Net Yards	253	242
Net Yards Rushing	188	87
Net Yards Passing	65	155
Passes (Att/Comp/Int)	20-9-0	26-11-1
Punts Average	8-38.9	6-35.7
Fumbles Lost	1-1	2-0
Penalties-Yards	7-70	8-66

INDIVIDUAL STATISTICS

Rushing

BEARS—Payton 28-192; Suhey 4-6; Gault 1-0; McMahon 4-(−10).

PACKERS—Ivery 9-26; Clark 17-58; Zorn 1-0; Lofton 1-3.

Passing

BEARS—McMahon 9-20, 91, 1 TD.

PACKERS—Zorn 11-26, 179, 1 TD.

Receiving

BEARS—Suhey 1-16; Moorehead 1-21; Wrightman 2-29; Payton 3-14; Perry 1-4; McKinnon 1-7.

PACKERS—Coffman 3-48; Epps 2-38; Ivery 2-22; Lofton 1-9; Clark 3-62.

Bears 24, Detroit Lions 3

at Soldier Field—November 10

Lions	0	0	3	0	— 3
Bears	7	7	7	3	— 24

BEARS—Fuller 1 run (Butler kick); BEARS—Thomas 7 run (Butler kick); LIONS—FG Murray 34; BEARS—Fuller 5 run (Butler kick); BEARS—FG Butler 39.

TEAM STATISTICS

	Bears	Lions
First Downs	26	8
Total Net Yards	360	106
Net Yards Rushing	250	68
Net Yards Passing	110	38
Passes (Att/Comp/Int)	13-7-0	17-8-2
Punts Average	2-20.5	3-30.7
Fumbles Lost	3-2	3-2
Penalties-Yards	5-40	6-31

INDIVIDUAL STATISTICS

Rushing

BEARS—Payton 26-107; Suhey 16-102; Gault 1-11; Gentry 2-13; Fuller 5-11; Thomas 4-13; Margerum 1-(−7).

LIONS—Hipple 2-(−2); J. Jones 19-68; Moore 1-2.

Passing

BEARS—Fuller 7-13, 112; Tomczak 0-0.

LIONS—Hipple 8-17, 73.

Receiving

BEARS—Margerum 1-8; Payton 4-69; Suhey 1-12; Wrightman 1-23.

LIONS—Rubick 1-18; Nichols 2-14; J. Jones 2-7; Mandley 2-20; Moore 1-14.

Bears 44, Dallas Cowboys 0

at Texas Stadium—November 17

Bears	7	17	3	17	— 44
Cowboys	0	0	0	0	— 0

BEARS—Dent 1 interception return (Butler kick); FG Butler 44; Richardson 36 interception return (Butler kick); Fuller 1 run (Butler kick); FG Butler 46; FG Butler 22; Thomas 16 run (Butler kick); Gentry 16 run (Butler kick).

TEAM STATISTICS

	Bears	Cowboys
First Downs	18	12
Total Net Yards	378	171
Net Yards Rushing	216	52
Net Yards Passing	162	119
Passes (Att/Comp/Int)	25-10-1	39-15-4
Punts Average	6-43.5	10-37.8
Fumbles Lost	1-0	1-1
Penalties-Yards	8-10.5	6-6.5

INDIVIDUAL STATISTICS
Rushing
BEARS—Payton 22-132; Gentry 3-24; Fuller 4-21; Thomas 4-19; Suhey 4-11; Perry 1-1; Sanders 2-8.
COWBOYS—Dorsett 12-44; Hogeboom 1-8; Lavette 3-0.
Passing
BEARS—Fuller 9-24, 164; Tomczak 0-0; Payton 1-1, 33.
COWBOYS—D. White 9-17, 107; Hogeboom 6-22, 60.
Receiving
BEARS—Wrightman 2-61; Suhey 2-46; Gault 2-24; McKinnon 1-24; Gentry 1-22; Moorehead 1-16; Payton 1-4.
COWBOYS—Renfro 3-45; Newsome 3-25; Cosbie 2-25; Hill 2-15; Cornwell 1-32; Dorsett 2-12; Fowler 1-9; Gonzalez 1-4.

Bears 36, Atlanta Falcons 0
at Soldier Field — November 24

Falcons	0 0 0 0 — 0
Bears	0 20 7 9 — 36

BEARS—FG Butler 35; FG Butler 32; Payton 40 run (Butler kick); Perry 1 run (Butler kick); Thomas 2 run (Butler kick); Waechter tackled Holly in end zone; Sanders 1 run (Butler kick).

TEAM STATISTICS

	Bears	Falcons
First Downs	24	10
Total Net Yards	379	119
Net Yards Rushing	196	141
Net Yards Passing	183	−22
Passes (Att/Comp/Int)	25-11-0	17-3-2
Punts Average	4-37.5	7-38.4
Fumbles Lost	1-1	1-1
Penalties-Yards	5-45	9-82

INDIVIDUAL STATISTICS
Rushing
BEARS—Payton 20-102; Suhey 2-4; Thomas 6-26; Fuller 2-11; Perry 1-1; Gentry 6-30; Tomczak 1-3; Sanders 5-19.
FALCONS—Riggs 30-110; Archer 3-19; J. Washington 3-12; Austin 1-0.
Passing
BEARS—Fuller 10-20, 151; Tomczak 2-4, 33.
FALCONS—Archer 2-15, 10; Holly 1-2, 6.
Receiving
BEARS—Moorehead 2-39; McKinnon 1-6; Payton 3-20; Wrightman 3-40; Gault 2-70; Sanders 1-9; Gentry 1-12.
FALCONS—Riggs 1-1; Cox 2-15.

Bears 24, Miami Dolphins 38
at Miami Orange Bowl — December 2

Bears	7 3 14 0 — 24
Miami	10 21 7 0 — 38

MIAMI—Moore 33 pass from Marino (Reveiz kick); BEARS—Fuller 1 run (Butler kick); MIAMI—FG Reveiz 47; MIAMI—Davenport 1 run (Reveiz kick); BEARS—FG Butler 30; MIAMI—Davenport 1 run (Reveiz kick); MIAMI—Moore 6 pass from Marino (Reveiz kick); BEARS—Fuller 1 run (Butler kick); MIAMI—Clayton 42 pass from Marino (Reveiz kick); BEARS—Margerum 19 pass from Fuller (Butler kick).

TEAM STATISTICS

	Bears	Miami
First Downs	23	17
Total Net Yards	343	335
Net Yards Rushing	167	90
Net Yards Passing	176	245
Passes (Att/Comp/Int)	28-14-3	27-14-1
Punts Average	3-29.0	3-44.7
Fumbles Lost	1-1	2-1
Penalties-Yards	7-65	6-61

INDIVIDUAL STATISTICS

Rushing
BEARS—Payton 23-121; Suhey 7-19; Fuller 6-19; McMahon 1-8.
MIAMI—Davenport 3-2; Bennett 5-12; Nathan 15-74; Hampton 1-2.
Passing
BEARS—Fuller 11-21, 169, 1 TD; Payton 0-1; McMahon 3-6, 42.
MIAMI—Marino 14-27, 270, 3 TDs.
Receiving
BEARS—Gault 2-79; Moorehead 4-33; Payton 2-16; Wrightman 1-12; Margerum 4-61; Gentry 1-10.
MIAMI—Moore 4-75; Duper 5-107; Clayton 5-88.

Bears 17, Indianapolis Colts 10
at Soldier Field — December 8

Colts	0 3 0 7 — 10
Bears	0 3 7 7 — 17

BEARS—FG Butler 20; COLTS—FG Allegre 30; BEARS—Payton 16 run (Butler kick); BEARS—Thomas 3 run (Butler kick); COLTS—Capers 61 pass from Pagel (Allegre kick).

TEAM STATISTICS

	Bears	Colts
First Downs	22	10
Total Net Yards	328	232
Net Yards Rushing	191	99
Net Yards Passing	137	133
Passes (Att/Comp/Int)	23-11-0	24-10-0
Punts Average	4-43.5	4-49.5
Fumbles Lost	0-0	0-0
Penalties-Yards	5-45	3-25

INDIVIDUAL STATISTICS
Rushing
BEARS—Payton 26-111; Suhey 8-17; McMahon 5-36; Thomas 5-27.
COLTS—McMillan 13-61; Wonsley 7-42; Capers 1-(−4).
Passing
BEARS—McMahon 11-23, 145.
COLTS—Pagel 10-24, 143
Receiving
BEARS—Gentry 2-38; Moorehead 1-24; Payton 2-23; Gault 3-36; Margerum 1-71; Suhey 2-17.
COLTS—Beach 3-35; Bentley 1-16; Boyer 1-2; O. Williams 1-10; Bouza 2-16; McMillan 1-3; Capers 1-61.

Bears 19, New York Jets 6
at Giants Stadium — December 14

Bears	3 7 3 6 — 19
Jets	3 0 3 0 — 6

BEARS—FG Butler 18; JETS—FG Leahy 23; BEARS—Wrightman 7 pass from McMahon (Butler kick); JETS—FG Leahy 55; BEARS—FG Butler 31; BEARS—FG Butler 37; BEARS—FG Butler 21.

TEAM STATISTICS

	Bears	Jets
First Downs	20	11
Total Net Yards	319	159
Net Yards Rushing	116	70
Net Yards Passing	283	89
Passes (Att/Comp/Int)	31-15-1	26-12-0
Punts Average	7-36.1	6-36.8
Fumbles Lost	1-0	3-3
Penalties-Yards	5-46	5-45

INDIVIDUAL STATISTICS
Rushing
BEARS—Payton 28-53; Suhey 7-23; Gentry 2-22; McMahon 3-18.
JETS—McNeil 20-63; Hector 2-5; Paige 1-2.
Passing
BEARS—McMahon 15-31, 215, 1 TD.
JETS—O'Brien 12-26, 122.
Receiving
BEARS—Wrightman 4-37; Gault 3-46; Moorehead 2-17; McKinnon 3-27; Payton 1-65; Gentry 1-7; Suhey 1-16.
JETS—McNeil 3-42; Toon 3-20; Shuler 3-29; Walker 1-11; Klever 1-11; Hector 1-9.

Bears 37, Detroit Lions 17
at Pontiac Silverdome — December 22

Bears	3 3 10 21 — 37
Lions	3 0 7 7 — 17

BEARS—FG Butler 25; LIONS—FG Murray 42; BEARS—FG Butler 24; BEARS—Gentry 94 kickoff return (Butler kick); BEARS—FG Butler 21; LIONS—Lewis 2 pass from Hipple (Murray kick); BEARS—McMahon 14 run (Butler kick); BEARS—Rivera 5 fumble recovery return (Butler kick); LIONS—J. Jones 2 run (Murray kick); BEARS—Margerum 11 pass from McMahon (Butler kick).

TEAM STATISTICS

	Bears	Lions
First Downs	20	22
Total Net Yards	382	326
Net Yards Rushing	161	73
Net Yards Passing	221	253
Passes (Att/Comp/Int)	26-14-3	47-24-3
Punts Average	1-40	3-41
Fumbles Lost	2-1	4-4
Penalties-Yards	8-58	2-15

INDIVIDUAL STATISTICS
Rushing
BEARS—Payton 17-81; Suhey 6-46; McMahon 3-15; Gentry 3-15; Fuller 1-4; Thomas 1-0.
LIONS—J. Jones 16-74; Moore 5-(−1).
Passing
BEARS—McMahon 13-22, 194, 2 TDs; Tomczak 0-2; Fuller 0-1; Payton 1-1, 50.
LIONS—Hipple 22-44, 287, 1 TD; Ferguson 2-3, 11.
Receiving
BEARS—Payton 4-55; Suhey 3-21; Wrightman 2-37; Moorehead 2-33; Gault 1-50; McKinnon 1-37; Margerum 1-11.
LIONS—Thompson 9-101; Mandley 5-127; Bland 5-48; Lewis 3-14; Moore 1-7; J. Jones 1-1.

DIVISIONAL PLAYOFF
Bears 21, Giants 0
Soldier Field — January 5, 1986

Giants	0 0 0 0 — 0
Bears	7 0 14 0 — 21

BEARS—Gayle 5 punt return (Butler kick); McKinnon 23 pass from McMahon (Butler kick); McKinnon 20 pass from McMahon (Butler kick).

TEAM STATISTICS

	Bears	Giants
First Downs	17	10
Total Net Yards	363	181
Net Yards Rushing	147	32
Net Yards Passing	216	149
Passes (Att/Comp/Int)	21-11-0	35-14-0
Punts Average	6-37.3	9-38.1
Fumbles Lost	0-0	3-1
Penalties-Yards	2-20	4-25

INDIVIDUAL STATISTICS
Rushing
BEARS—Payton 27-93; Suhey 6-33; McMahon 5-18; Thomas 4-11; McKinnon 1-(−7); Gentry 1-(−1).
GIANTS—Morris 12-32; Williams 1-(−9); Galbreath 1-9.
Passing
BEARS—McMahon 11-21, 216, 2 TDs.
GIANTS—Simms 14-35, 209.
Receiving
BEARS—Payton 1-4; Gault 3-68; McKinnon 3-52; Suhey 2-5; Gentry 1-41; Wrightman 1-46.
GIANTS—Carpenter 3-24; Bavaro 4-36; Adams 3-65; Johnson 1-17; McConkey 1-23; Galbreath 1-11; B. Williams 1-33.

NFC CHAMPIONSHIP GAME
Bears 24, Rams 0
Soldier Field — January 12, 1986

LA Rams	0 0 0 0 — 0
Chicago Bears	10 0 7 7 — 24

BEARS—McMahon 16 run (Butler kick); FG Butler 34; Gault 22 pass from McMahon (Butler kick); Marshall 52 fumble return.

TEAM STATISTICS

	Bears	Rams
First Downs	9	13
Total Net Yards	232	130
Net Yards Rushing	91	86
Net Yards Passing	141	44
Passes (Att/Comp/Int)	25-16-0	31-10-1
Punts Average	10-36.2	11-39.2
Penalties-Yards	6-48	4-25

INDIVIDUAL STATISTICS
Rushing
BEARS—Payton 18-32; Suhey 6-23; McMahon 4-28; Gentry 2-9.
RAMS—Dickerson 17-46; Redden 9-40.
Passing
BEARS—McMahon 16-25, 164, 1 TD.
RAMS—Brock 10-31, 66.
Receiving
BEARS—Moorehead 2-28; Gault 4-56; Payton 7-48; Wrightman 3-44; Suhey 1-7; McKinnon 1-17.
RAMS—Hunter 3-29; Brown 2-14; Dickerson 3-10; Ellard 1-5; Duckworth 1-8.

BEARS, 1985 FINAL STATISTICS (16 Games)

TEAM STATISTICS

TEAM STATISTICS	BEARS	OPPONENT
TOTAL FIRST DOWNS	343	236
Rushing	176	74
Passing	145	141
Penalty	22	21
3rd Down: Made/Att.	85-219	61-205
4th Down: Made/Att.	5-13	6-16
TOTAL NET YARDS	5837	4135
Avg. Per Game	364.8	258.4
Total Plays	1085	945
Avg. Per Play	5.4	4.4
NET YARDS RUSHING	2761	1319
Avg. Per Game	172.6	82.4
Total Rushes	610	359
NET YARDS PASSING	3076	2816
Avg. Per Game	192.3	176.0
Tackled/Yards Lost	43-227	64-483
Gross Yards	3303	3299
Attempts/Completions	432-237	522-249
Pct. of Completions	54.9	47.7
Had Intercepted	16	34
PUNTS/AVERAGE	68-42.2	90-40.4
NET PUNTING AVG.	35.1	33.5
PENALTIES/YARDS	104-912	115-934
FUMBLES/BALL LOST	24-15	30-20
TOUCHDOWNS	51	23
Rushing	27	6
Passing	17	16
Returns	7	1

SCORE BY PERIODS

	1	2	3	4	OT	Total
BEARS TOTAL	67	144	123	122	0	456
Opp. Total	50	77	34	37	0	198

SCORING

SCORING	TDR	TDP	TDRt	PAT	FG	S	TP
Butler	0	0	0	51-51	31-38	0	144
Payton	9	2	0	0-0	0-0	0	66
McKinnon	0	7	0	0-0	0-0	0	42
Fuller	5	0	0	0-0	0-0	0	30
McMahon	3	1	0	0-0	0-0	0	24
Thomas	4	0	0	0-0	0-0	0	24
Gentry	2	0	1	0-0	0-0	0	18
Perry	2	1	0	0-0	0-0	0	18
Suhey	1	1	0	0-0	0-0	0	12
Margerum	0	2	0	0-0	0-0	0	12
Gault	0	1	1	0-0	0-0	0	12
Wilson	0	0	1	0-0	0-0	1	8
Dent	0	0	1	0-0	0-0	0	6
Frazier	0	0	1	0-0	0-0	0	6
Wrightman	0	1	0	0-0	0-0	0	6
Rivera	0	0	1	0-0	0-0	0	6
Moorehead	0	1	0	0-0	0-0	0	6
Sanders	1	0	0	0-0	0-0	0	6
Richardson	0	0	1	0-0	0-0	0	6
Waechter	0	0	0	0-0	0-0	1	2
McMichael	0	0	0	0-0	0-0	1	2
BEARS TOTAL	27	17	7	51-51	31-38	3	456
Opp. Total	6	16	1	22-23	12-19	1	1

FIELD GOALS

FIELD GOALS	1-19	20-29	30-39	40-49	50+	Total
Butler	2-2	13-13	13-14	3-6	0-3	31-38
BEARS TOTAL	2-2	13-13	13-14	3-6	0-3	31-38
Opp. Total	1-1	2-3	5-6	3-5	1-4	12-19

FIELD GOALS: Made Missed
K. Butler (38, 63, 45) (21, 28) (24, 19, 34, 34, 31, 45) (28) (30, 30) (34, 38, 27, 29) () (40, 29) () (43, 39) (44, 46, 22) (35, 32) (30) (20) (18, 31, 37, 21) (25, 51, 24, 50, 21)

PASSING

PASSING	Att.	Comp.	Yards	Pct.	Avg. Att.	TD	Pct. TD	Int.	LG	Lost/Att.	Rating
McMahon	313	178	2392	56.9	7.64	15	4.8	11	70	28-125	82.8
Fuller	107	53	777	49.5	7.26	1	.9	5	69	17-102	57.0
Payton	5	3	96	60.0	19.20	1	20.0	0	50	0-0	143.8
Tomczak	6	2	33	33.3	5.50	0	.0	0	24	0-0	52.8
BEARS TOTAL	432	237	3303	54.9	7.65	17	3.9	16	70	43-227	77.3
Opp. Total	522	249	3299	47.7	6.32	16	3.1	34	90	64-483	51.4

RUSHING

RUSHING	No.	Yds.	Avg.	LG	TD
Payton	324	1551	4.8	40	9
Suhey	115	471	4.1	17	1
McMahon	47	252	5.4	19	3
Gentry	30	160	5.3	21	2
Thomas	31	125	4.0	17	4
Sanders	25	104	4.2	28	1
Fuller	24	77	3.2	19	5
Gault	5	18	3.6	11	0
Margerum	1	-7	-7.0	0	0
Perry	5	7	1.4	2	2
Tomczak	2	3	1.5	3	0
McKinnon	1	0	.0	0	0
BEARS TOTAL	610	2761	4.5	40	27
Opp. Total	359	1319	3.7	37	6

RECEIVING

RECEIVING	No.	Yds.	Avg.	LG	TD
Payton	49	483	9.9	65	2
Moorehead	35	481	13.7	25	1
Gault	33	704	21.3	70	1
Suhey	33	295	8.9	35	1
McKinnon	31	555	17.9	48	7
Wrightman	24	407	17.0	49	1
Margerum	17	190	11.2	20	2
Gentry	5	77	15.4	30	0
Thomas	5	45	9.0	15	0
Maness	1	34	34.0	34	0
McMahon	1	13	13	13	1
Anderson	1	6	6	6	0
Sanders	1	9	9	9	0
Perry	1	4	4	4	1
BEARS TOTAL	237	3303	13.9	70	17
Opp. Total	249	3299	13.2	90	16

INTERCEPTIONS

INTERCEPTIONS	No.	Yds.	Avg.	LG	TD
Frazier	6	119	19.8	33	1
Duerson	5	58	11.6	37	0
Fencik	5	38	7.6	22	0
Marshall	5	27	5.4	14	0
Richardson	4	174	43.5	90	1
Wilson	3	35	11.7	23	1
Taylor	3	28	9.3	18	0
Dent	2	10	5	9	1
Singletary	1	23	23	23	0
BEARS TOTAL	34	512	15.1	90	4
Opp. Total	46	99	2.2	43	1

PUNTING

PUNTING	No.	Yds.	Avg.	TB	In 20	LG	Blk.
Buford	68	2870	42.2	14	18	69	0
* Team	1	0	.0	0	0	0	1
BEARS TOTAL	69	2870	41.6	14	18	69	1
Opp. Total	90	3639	40.4	6	11	75	1

PUNT RETURNS

PUNT RETURNS	No.	FC	Yds.	Avg.	LG	TD
Taylor	25	8	198	7.9	21	0
Ortego	17	2	158	9.3	23	0
Duerson	6	0	47	7.8	11	0
Gentry	0	0	47	.0	47	0
Maness	2	0	44	11	11	0
McKinnon	4	0	9	4½	5	0
BEARS TOTAL	54	10	503	9.3	47	0
Opp. Total	24	9	203	8.5	29	0

KICKOFF RETURNS

KICKOFF RETURNS	No.	Yds.	Avg.	LG	TD
Gault	22	577	26.2	99	1
Gentry	18	466	25.9	94	1
Sanders	1	10	10.0	10	0
Taylor	1	18	18.0	18	0
Marshall	0	2	.0	2	0
McKinnon	1	16	16.0	16	0
BEARS TOTAL	43	1089	25.3	99	2
Opp. Total	78	1827	23.4	58	0

SUPER BOWL XX PLAY-BY-PLAY

First Quarter

Chicago wins the toss. Elects to receive.
Franklin kicks to Gault at Chicago 8-yard line. Returns to Chicago 18.
Chicago 15:00
1-10, C18: Payton left tackle for 7 (Nelson).
2-3, C25: Payton fumbled, forced by Veris, recovered by McGrew on 19.
New England 14:01
1-10, C19: Eason left sideline pass intended for Dawson, incomplete.
2-10, C19: Eason pass over middle intended for Morgan, incomplete, broken up by Singletary.
3-10, C19: Eason pass in right end zone intended for Starring, out of bounds.
4-10, C19: Franklin 36-yard field goal.
NEW ENGLAND 3, CHICAGO 0
Franklin kicks out of bounds on left sideline on 12. 5-yard penalty.
Franklin kicks from 30 to Chicago 13. Gault returns to 31.
Chicago 13:41
1-10, C31: McMahon pass to left flat intended for Moorehead, incomplete, broken up by Blackmon.
2-10, C31: McMahon 43 pass to Gault on right sideline (Gibson).
1-10, NE26: Suhey 7 run middle (Tippett).
2-3 NE19: Suhey 5 run middle (McGrew).
1-10, NE14: Payton 1 run right tackle (Tippett, Nelson).
2-9, NE13: McMahon pass to left flat intended for Payton, incomplete, tipped by Blackmon.
3-9, NE13: McMahon 3 run (Lippett).
4-6, NE10: Butler 28-yard field goal.
NEW ENGLAND 3, CHICAGO 3
Butler kicks to 5. Starring returns to 41 (Ortego).
New England 9:20
1-10, NE41: Eason incomplete pass over the middle, intended for Starring, overthrown.
2-10, NE41: Eason incomplete pass to left flat, dropped by Morgan.
3-10, NE41: Eason sacked for loss of 10 (Marshall, Wilson).
4-20, NE31: Camarillo punts to Ortego on 21, return to 29 (Tatupu).
Chicago 8:18
1-10, C29: McMahon 19 pass to Gault at right sideline (Lippett).
1-10, C48: McMahon incomplete pass thrown out of bounds on right sideline, intended for Suhey.
2-10, C48: McMahon runs out of pocket, loss of 3 (Blackmon).
3-13, C45: Payton 3 run right tackle (Nelson).
4-10, C48: Buford 52 punt into end zone. Touchback.
New England 5:59
1-10, NE20: C. James up the middle for no gain (Singletary).
2-10, NE20: Eason sacked by Dent and McMichael, fumble recovered by Hampton on NE13.
Chicago 5:17
1-10, NE13: McMahon rolls right, 8 pass to Moorehead left side.
2-2, NE5: Payton 1 run middle.
3-1, NE4: McMahon 1 run middle (Nelson).
1-G, NE3: Payton loss of 2 left end (Blackmon).
2-G, NE5: Perry right sweep loss of 1 (Owens, Thomas).
3-G, NE6: McMahon incomplete pass intended for Thomas in left flat.
4-G, NE6: Butler 24-yard field goal.
CHICAGO 6, NEW ENGLAND 3
Butler kicks off to Starring on New England 6. Returns to New England 17 (Marshall).
New England 1:26
1-10, NE18: C. James run left tackle, fumble forced by Dent, recovered by Singletary on New England 13.
Chicago 1:10
1-10, NE13: Suhey 2 run middle (Adams).
2-8, NE11: Suhey 11 TD run right tackle. Offsides penalty on New England declined. Butler PAT.
CHICAGO 13, NEW ENGLAND 3
Butler kicks to Starring on New England 8. Returns to 24.
New England 0:23
1-10, NE24: C. James 3 run left tackle (Perry).

Second Quarter

2-7, NE27: Eason incomplete pass to right sideline intended for Morgan, tipped by Richardson.
3-7, NE27: Hawthorne loss of 4 middle (Dent).
4-11, NE23: Camarillo 43 punt return by Ortego 2 yards to Chicago 41.
Chicago 14:01
1-10, C41: Thomas 1 run left side (Nelson).
2-9, C42: McMahon 4 pass over the middle to Thomas (McGrew, Tippett).
3-5, C46: Gentry 8 run left side (Clayborn).
1-10, NE46: McMahon 7 pass right flat to Gault (Lippett).
2-3, NE39: McMahon 24 pass left sideline to Suhey (Clayborn).
1-10, NE15: Suhey 7 run off right tackle (Marion).
2-3, NE8: Suhey 1 run left tackle (Veris).
3-2, NE7: Suhey 3 run up middle (McGrew).
CHICAGO TIME OUT
1-G, NE4: Payton 2 run up middle (Veris, Owens).
CHICAGO TIME OUT
2-G, NE2: McMahon 2 TD run up middle. Butler PAT.
CHICAGO 20, NEW ENGLAND 3
Butler kicks to New England 10. Starring return to 29 (Rivera).
New England 7:24
1-10, NE29: C. James up middle no gain (Dent).
2-10, NE29: Collins loss of 2 right side (Marshall).
3-12, NE27: Eason sacked loss of 11 (Wilson, McMichael).
4-23, NE16: Camarillo 39 punt to Chicago 47. Ortego illegal fair catch, 5-yard penalty accepted by New England.
Chicago 5:21.
1-10, C42: Payton 5 run left sideline, driven out of bounds by Blackmon.
2-5, C47: Suhey no gain left tackle, fumble forced by Blackmon recovered by Clayborn on New England 46.
New England 5:08
1-10, NE46: Grogan pass intended for Morgan at left sideline blocked by Dent.
2-10, NE46: Grogan 8 pass right flat to Collins (Richardson).
3-2, C46: Grogan 6 pass left flat to C. James (Fencik, Perry).
1-10, C40: Collins 3 run right side (Hampton).
2-7, C37: Grogan incomplete pass right sideline intended for Ramsey, overthrown.
3-7, C37: Grogan incomplete pass right sideline intended for Morgan, overthrown.
4-7, C37: Camarillo 17 punt out of bounds on Chicago 20.
Chicago 2:58
1-10, C20: Payton 6 run left side (Adams).
2-4, C26: Payton 6 run right side (Tippett).
TWO-MINUTE WARNING
1-10, C32: Payton 3 run middle (Veris).
2-7, C35: McMahon incomplete pass left sideline intended for Wrightman, overthrown. 5-yard illegal use of hands penalty on New England's Lippett accepted.
1-10, C40: McMahon incomplete pass left sideline intended for Wrightman, overthrown.
2-10, C40: McMahon pass right sideline blocked by Tippett.
3-10, C40: McMahon 14 pass over middle to Gentry (Gibson).
1-10, NE46: Gentry 5 run on draw (Veris).
2-5, NE41: McMahon 29 pass over middle to Margerum (R. James).
CHICAGO TIME OUT
1-10, NE12: Gentry 2 run on draw (Blackmon).
2-8, NE10: McMahon 7 run right tackle (Marion).
3-1, NE3: Chicago 5-yard illegal procedure penalty.
3-6, NE8: Butler 25-yard field goal.

Third Quarter

Butler kicks off to New England 5-yard line. Starring returns to New England 22.
New England 15:00
1-10, NE22: Grogan 8 pass left sideline to Morgan (Phillips).
2-2, NE30: Collins 3 run middle (Marshall).
1-10, NE33: Grogan sacked for loss of 5 (McMichael, Dent).
2-15, NE28: 5-yard false start penalty on New England's Wooten accepted.
2-20, NE23: Grogan sacked for loss of 13 (Wilson, Hampton).
3-33, NE10: Grogan 24 pass to Starring right sideline (Duerson).
4-9, NE34: Camarillo 62 punt downed on Chicago 4.
Chicago 12:27
1-10, C4: McMahon 60 pass right sideline to Gault (Marion).
1-10, NE36: McMahon 14 pass left sideline to Moorehead.
1-10, NE22: Payton 2 run left tackle (Nelson).
2-8, NE20: Payton 4 run right sweep (Tippett).
3-4, NE16: Suhey 4 run middle (Veris).
1-10, NE12: Suhey 4 run left sweep (Adams).
2-6, NE8: McMahon incomplete pass right flat intended for McKinnon, broken up by Lippett.
3-6, NE8: McMahon 7 pass right flat to Margerum (R. James).
1-G, NE1: McMahon 1 TD run middle. Butler PAT.
CHICAGO 30, NEW ENGLAND 3
15-yard facemask penalty on New England, Chicago will kick off from 50.
Butler kicks off into end zone. Ball downed. Touchback.
New England 7:22
1-10, NE20: Grogan incomplete left screen pass to C. James.
2-10, NE20: C. James 3 run right sweep.
3-7, NE23: Grogan pass tipped by Ramsey intercepted at 28 by Phillips, returned for TD. Butler PAT.
CHICAGO 37, NEW ENGLAND 3
Butler kicks off to New England 6-yard line. Starring returns to New England 31.
New England 6:16
1-10, NE31: Grogan incomplete fly pass over middle intended for Morgan, batted away by Richardson.
2-10, NE31: Grogan 14 pass to C. James, fumble recovered by Marshall on 50, returned to 40 lateraled to Wilson to 37 (C. James).
Chicago 5:43
1-10, NE37: Payton 6 run right side.
2-4, NE31: Payton 7 run right side.
1-10, NE24: Payton loss of 4 right side.
2-14, NE28: McMahon incomplete pass right flat intended for Payton.
3-14, NE28: McMahon 27 pass to Gentry right sideline out of bounds at 1.
1-G, NE1: Perry 1 TD run left tackle. Butler PAT good.
CHICAGO 44, NEW ENGLAND 3
Butler kicks off to New England 4-yard line. Starring returns to New England 24.
New England 3:22
1-10, NE24: Grogan 15 pass to Starring right sideline (Richardson).
1-10, NE39: Grogan 13 pass to Morgan left sideline (Phillips).
1-10, C48: Grogan incomplete fly pass intended for Starring, batted away by Richardson. 5-yard offsides penalty on Chicago accepted.
1-5, C43: Weathers 3 run middle (McMichael).
2-2, C40: Grogan 11 pass left flat to Ramsey.
1-10, C29: Grogan 3 run middle.
2-7, C26: Grogan incomplete pass over middle intended for Morgan, batted away by Richardson. 5-yard illegal procedure on Chicago accepted.
2-2, C21: Grogan 3 pass to Weathers left sideline (Marshall).
1-10, C18: Grogan sacked for loss of 10 (Hampton).

Fourth Quarter

2-20, C28: Grogan incomplete pass intended for Tatupu right flat. 10-yard illegal use of hands penalty on Chicago's Wilson accepted.
1-10, C23: Grogan 16 pass to Morgan left sideline (Phillips).
1-G, C17: Grogan incomplete pass intended to Tatupu, overthrown.
2-G, C7: Grogan loss of 1 pass to Morgan (Richardson).
3-G, C8: Grogan incomplete pass to Morgan left side.
4-G, C8: Grogan 8 TD pass to Fryar. Franklin PAT.
CHICAGO 44, NEW ENGLAND 10.
Franklin kicks off to Chicago 8-yard line. Gault returns to Chicago 24.
Chicago 13:14.
1-10, C24: Payton 7 run left side (R. James).
2-3, C31: Payton 1 run left side (Owens).
3-2, C32: Payton 1 gain left sweep (R. James).
4-1, C33: Buford 41 punt to New England 26-yard line. Fryar returns to New England 38 (Dawson).
New England 11:23
1-10, NE38: Grogan 5 pass to Ramsey over middle, fumble forced by Gayle, recovered by Singletary on New England 43.
Chicago 11:16
1-10, NE43: Fuller incomplete pass over the middle to Margerum.
2-10, NE43: Payton 3 run right side (Lippett).
3-7, NE40: Fuller incomplete pass right flat to Payton.
4-7, NE40: Buford 36 punt to New England 4, downed by Thrift on New England 4.
New England 10:06
1-10, NE4: Grogan incomplete fly pass intended for Fryar, overthrown.
2-10, NE4: Grogan 15 left screen pass to Morgan (Rivera).
1-10, NE19: Grogan 11 right screen pass to Collins (Phillips).
1-10, NE30: Grogan 16 left sideline to Fryar.
1-10, NE46: Grogan right sideline pass intercepted by Morrissey at Chicago 48 returned to New England 5.
Chicago 7:57
1-G, NE5: Payton 1 run middle (Thomas, Blackmon).
2-G, NE4: Payton 2 run left side (Nelson). 10-yard illegal block penalty on Chicago's Moorehead accepted.
2-G, NE14: Fuller incomplete pass intended for Margerum in end zone, broken up by Lippett. 5-yard illegal pass by Fuller, thrown from 13-yard line accepted. Loss of down.
3-G, NE18: Thomas 7 run middle (Marlon, Tippett).
4-G, NE11: Payton 6 run on draw (Owens). Chicago loses possession.
New England 5:48
1-10, NE5: Grogan incomplete pass left sideline intended for Starring, broken up by Phillips.
2-10, NE5: Grogan sacked in end zone (Waechter). Safety.
CHICAGO 46, NEW ENGLAND 10.
Camarillo free kicks from New England 20 to Chicago 24. Gault returns to Chicago 28.
Chicago 5:36
1-10, C28: Fuller sacked for loss of 11 (Thomas).
2-21, C17: Fuller incomplete pass left sideline intended for Wrightman, overthrown.
3-21, C17: Fuller incomplete pass right sideline intended for Gentry, overthrown.
4-21, C17: Buford 44-punt to New England 39-yard line. Fryar returns to New England 49. Facemask penalty on Chicago, illegal block on New England. Offsetting penalties.
New England 4:28
1-10, NE49: Grogan no gain pass left sideline to Morgan (Duerson).
2-10, NE49: Grogan incomplete right flat pass intended for Morgan, thrown short.
3-10, NE49: Grogan incomplete pass over middle intended for Fryar, overthrown.
4-10, NE49: Camarillo 51-yard punt into Chicago end zone. Touchback.
Chicago 3:30
1-10, C20: Sanders 3 run middle (Reynolds).
2-7, C23: Suhey no gain middle (Rembert). 5-yard offsides penalty on New England accepted.
2-2, C28: Suhey 7 run left sweep (Marion).
TWO-MINUTE WARNING
1-10, C35: Sanders 6 run left side (Thomas, Marion).
2-4, C41: Sanders 11 run up middle (Marion).
1-10, NE49: Sanders loss of 5 left sweep (Ingram).

SUPER BOWL XX
HOW THEY SCORED

Chicago	13	10	21	2—	46
New England	3	0	0	7—	10

HOW THEY SCORED

FIRST QUARTER

New England—FG Franklin 36, 1:19. 4 plays, 0 yards. Key Play: McGrew recovery of Payton fumble on Chicago 19.
New England 3, Chicago 0

Chicago—FG Butler 28, 5:40. 59 yards, 8 plays. Key Play: McMahon 43 pass to Gault.
New England 3, Chicago 3

Chicago—FG Butler 24, 13:39. 7 yards, 7 plays. Key Play: Hampton recovery of Eason fumble on New England 13.
Chicago 6, New England 3

Chicago—Suhey 11 run (Butler kick), 14:37. 13 yards, 2 plays. Key Play: Singletary recovery of C. James fumble on New England 13.
Chicago 13, New England 3

SECOND QUARTER

Chicago—McMahon, 2 run (Butler kick), 7:36. 59 yards, 10 plays. Key Play: McMahon 24 pass to Suhey.
Chicago 20, New England 3

Chicago—FG Butler 25, 15:00. 72 yards, 11 plays. Key Plays: McMahon 14 pass to Gentry on 3rd and 10; McMahon 29 pass to Margerum.
Chicago 23, New England 3

THIRD QUARTER

Chicago—McMahon 1 run (Butler kick), 7:38. 96 yards, 9 plays. Key Plays: McMahon 60 pass to Gault; McMahon 7 pass to Margerum on 3rd and 6.
Chicago 30, New England 3

Chicago—Phillips 28 interception return (Butler kick), 8:44.
Chicago 37, New England 3

Chicago—Perry 1 run (Butler kick), 11:38. 37 yards, 6 plays. Key Plays: Marshall recovery of C. James fumble at 50, returned by Marshall and Wilson to 37; McMahon 27 pass to Gentry on 3rd and 14.
Chicago 44, New England 3

FOURTH QUARTER

New England—Fryar 8 pass from Grogan (Franklin kick), 1:46. 76 yards, 15 plays. Key Plays: Grogan 15 pass to Starring; Grogan 21 pass to Morgan.
Chicago 44, New England 10

Chicago—Safety, Grogan tackled in end zone by Waechter, 9:24.
Chicago 46, New England 10

ATTENDANCE—73,818.

TEAM STATISTICS

CHICAGO		NEW ENGLAND
23	First downs	12
13	Rushing	1
9	Passing	10
1	Penalty	1
7-14	Third-down conversions	1-10
76	Offensive plays	54
408	Total yards	123
5.4	Yards per play	2.3
49-167	Rushes/yards	11-7
3.4	Gain per rush	1.6
241	Pass yards	116
10.0	Gain per pass	3.2
24-12	Attempted/Completed	36-17
0	Had intercepted	2
7-61	Sacks by	3-15
144	Return yards	175
2-20	Punts	2-22
4-49	Kickoffs	7-153
2-75	Interceptions	0-0
3-2	Fumbles/lost	4-4
4-43	Punts	6-44
6-35	Penalties/yards	5-35
5	Touchdowns	1
4	Rushing	0
0	Passing	1
1	Returns	0
3/3	Field goals	1/1
39:15	Possession time	20:45

INDIVIDUAL STATISTICS

Chicago Rushing

Player	No	Yds	Avg	Lg	Td
Payton	22	61	2.8	7	0
Suhey	11	52	4.7	11	1
Gentry	3	15	5.0	8	0
Sanders	4	15	3.8	11	0
McMahon	5	14	2.8	7	2
Thomas	2	8	4.0	7	0
Perry	1	1	1.0	1	1
Fuller	1	1	1.0	1	0
Totals	49	167	3.4	11	4

New England Rushing

Player	No	Yds	Avg	Lg	Td
Collins	3	4	1.3	3	0
Weathers	1	3	3.0	3	0
Grogan	1	3	3.0	3	0
James	5	1	0.2	3	0
Hawthorne	1	−4	−4.0	−4	0
Totals	11	7	0.6	3	0

Chicago Receiving

Player	No	Yds	Avg	Lg	Td
Gault	4	129	32.3	60	0
Gentry	2	41	20.5	27	0
Margerum	2	36	18.0	29	0
Moorehead	2	22	11.0	14	0
Suhey	1	24	24.0	24	0
Thomas	1	4	4.0	4	0
Totals	12	256	21.3	60	0

New England Receiving

Player	No	Yds	Avg	Lg	Td
Morgan	7	70	10.0	16	0
Starring	2	39	19.5	24	0
Fryar	2	24	12.0	16	1
Collins	2	19	9.5	11	0
Ramsey	2	16	8.0	11	0
James	1	6	6.0	6	0
Weathers	1	3	3.0	3	0
Totals	17	177	10.4	24	1

Chicago Passing

Player	Att	Cmp	Yds	Pct	Td	Int
McMahon	20	12	256	.600	0	0
Fuller	4	0	0	.000	0	0
Totals	24	12	256	.500	0	0

New England Passing

Player	Att	Cmp	Yds	Pct	Td	Int
Eason	6	0	0	.000	0	0
Grogan	30	17	177	.567	1	2
Totals	36	17	177	.472	1	2

Chicago Field Goals

Player	20-29	30-39	40-49	Tot
Butler	3/3	0/0	0/0	3/3

New England Field Goals

Player	20-29	30-39	40-49	Tot
Franklin	0/0	1/1	0/0	1/1

OFFICIALS — Red Cashion, referee; Ron Botchan, umpire; Jack Vaughan, field judge; Dale Williams, head linesman; Bama Glass, line judge; Bob Wright, side judge; Al Jury, back judge.

NFL 1985 INDIVIDUAL LEADERS

NFL TOP 10 RUSHERS

	Att.	Yds.	Avg.	LG	TD
Marcus Allen, L.A. Raiders	380	1759	4.6	61t	11
Gerald Riggs, Atlanta	397	1719	4.3	50	10
Walter Payton, Chicago	324	1551	4.8	40t	9
Joe Morris, N.Y. Giants	294	1336	4.5	65t	21
Freeman McNeil, N.Y. Jets	294	1331	4.5	69	3
Tony Dorsett, Dallas	305	1307	4.3	60t	7
James Wilder, Tampa Bay	365	1300	3.6	28	10
Eric Dickerson, L.A. Rams	292	1234	4.2	43	12
James Craig, New England	263	1227	4.7	65t	5
Kevin Mack, Cleveland	222	1104	5.0	61	7

NFL TOP 10 INTERCEPTORS

	No.	Yds.	Avg.	LG	TD
Everson Walls, Dallas	9	31	3.4	19	0
Albert Lewis, Kansas City	8	59	7.4	16	0
Eugene Daniel, Indianapolis	8	53	6.6	29	0
Fred Marion, New England	7	189	27.0	83	0
James Griffin, Cincinnati	7	116	16.6	33	1
Deron Cherry, Kansas City	7	87	12.4	47t	1
Charles Romes, Buffalo	7	56	8.0	21	0
Jeremiah Castille, Tampa Bay	7	49	7.0	20	0
John Harris, Seattle	7	20	2.9	17	0
11 players tied	6	—	—	—	—

NFL TOP 10 PASS RECEIVERS

	No.	Yds.	Avg.	LG	TD
Roger Craig, San Francisco	92	1016	11.0	73	6
Art Monk, Washington	91	1226	13.5	53	2
Lionel James, San Diego	86	1027	11.9	67t	6
Todd Christensen, L.A. Raiders	82	987	12.0	48	6
Butch Woolfolk, Houston	80	814	10.2	80t	4
Steve Largent, Seattle	79	1287	16.3	43	6
Mickey Shuler, N.Y. Jets	76	879	11.6	35	7
John Stallworth, Pittsburgh	75	937	12.5	41	5
Tony Hill, Dallas	74	1113	15.0	53t	7
Mike Quick, Philadelphia	73	1247	17.1	99t	11

NFL TOP 10 PUNT RETURNERS

	No.	FC	Yds.	Avg.	LG	TD
Irving Fryar, New England	37	15	520	14.1	85t	2
Henry Ellard, L.A. Rams	37	9	501	13.5	80t	1
Louis Lipps, Pittsburgh	36	2	437	12.1	71t	2
Fulton Walker, L.A. Raiders	62	6	692	11.2	32	0
Robbie Martin, Indianapolis	40	7	443	11.1	70t	1
J.T. Smith, St. Louis	26	10	283	10.9	31	0
Pete Mandley, Detroit	38	5	403	10.6	63t	1
Ken Jenkins, Washington	26	9	272	10.5	28	0
Paul Skansi, Seattle	31	7	312	10.1	32	0
Willie Drewrey, Houston	24	10	215	9.0	23	0

NFL TOP 10 PASSERS

	Att.	Comp.	Pct. Comp.	Yards	Avg. Gain	TD	Pct. TD	LG	Int.	Pct. Int.	Rating Points
Ken O'Brien, N.Y. Jets	488	297	60.9	3883	7.97	25	5.1	96t	8	1.6	96.2
Boomer Esiason, Cincinnati	431	251	58.2	3443	7.99	27	6.3	68t	12	2.8	93.2
Joe Montana, San Francisco	494	303	61.3	3653	7.39	27	5.5	73	13	2.6	91.3
Dan Fouts, San Diego	430	254	59.1	3638	8.46	27	6.3	75t	20	4.7	88.1
Dan Marino, Miami	567	336	59.3	4137	7.30	30	5.3	73	21	3.7	84.1
Bill Kenney, Kansas City	338	181	53.6	2536	7.50	17	5.0	84t	9	2.7	83.6
Jim McMahon, Chicago	313	178	56.9	2392	7.64	15	4.8	70t	11	3.5	82.6
Dieter Brock, L.A. Rams	365	218	59.7	2658	7.28	16	4.4	64t	13	3.6	82.0
Danny White, Dallas	450	267	59.3	3157	7.02	21	4.7	56t	17	3.8	80.6
Neil Lomax, St. Louis	471	265	56.3	3214	6.82	18	3.8	47	12	2.5	79.5

PHOTO CREDITS

Tim Alexander 171 (bottom)
Bob Allen 49, 174, 183
John Biever 17
Vernon Biever 39, 58, 97, 99
Jim Chaffin 82
Tom Croke 57, 140-141, 152
Dave Cross 92, 93
Scott Cunningham 2-3, 8, 21, 83, 161, 165, 173
Jonathan Daniel 61, 98, 116
Bruce Dierdorff 68, 103
Brian Drake 25 (right), 27, 41, 50-51, 79
Gin Ellis 177, 179
Malcolm Emmons 6, 131 (top) 175
L.D. Fullerton 64-65, 131 (bottom)
Richard Gentile 70-71
George Gojkovich 77, 112
Pete J. Groh 74, 124, 125, 130
Paul Jasienski 55, 99, 144
Trevor Jones for Allsport 23
Rick Kolodziej 62, 63
Don Lansu 56, 85, 104, 105, 117
John McDonough 13, 162
Al Messerschmidt 1, 10, 33, 35, 37, 67, 69,
    81, 88, 123, 136, 137, 167, 169, 182, 192
Peter Read Miller 170, 171 (top), 181
Vic Milton 107
Jerry Pinkus 45, 156
George Robarge 154
Bob Rosato 122, 150
Ron Ross 89
Betsy Peabody Rowe 139
Manny Rubio 19, 29, 178 (bottom)
Alan Schwartz 110, 111, 121, 159
Rebecca Skelton 109
Chuck Solomon 73
Paul Spinelli 113, 147
Dave Stock 94-95
Damian Strohmeyer 46, 106, 115
Steve Swope 128
Tony Tomsic 15, 25 (left), 75, 31, 43, 178 (top)
Corky Trewin 100-101
Jim Turner 133, 149
Ron Veseley 127, 129
Herb Weitman 76
Ror. Wyatt 134-135
Michael Yada 118-119
Hank Young 86-87, 142-143
Michael Zagaris 4-5, 52, 53, 80

Portrait of Victory was printed
by R.R. Donnelley, Willard, Ohio
on 70# Warren Webflo.
Color separations by American Color,
Santa Ana, California.
Helvetica Ultra Compressed, display
heads composed by Capco, California
Phototypography Company, Los Angeles.
Text typography was set in ITC Century
Book Condensed, by Rick Wadholm
and Marilyn Arai at NFLP Creative
Services, Los Angeles.